Individuals and Small Groups in Jewish Resistance to the Holocaust

Individuals and Small Groups in Jewish Resistance to the Holocaust

A Case Study of a Young Couple and Their Friends

Ben Braber

ANTHEM PRESS

Anthem Press
An imprint of Wimbledon Publishing Company
www.anthempress.com

This edition first published in UK and USA 2023
by ANTHEM PRESS
75–76 Blackfriars Road, London SE1 8HA, UK
or PO Box 9779, London SW19 7ZG, UK
and
244 Madison Ave #116, New York, NY 10016, USA

Copyright © Ben Braber 2023

The author asserts the moral right to be identified as the author of this work.

All rights reserved. Without limiting the rights under copyright reserved above, no part of this publication may be reproduced, stored or introduced into a retrieval system, or transmitted, in any form or by any means (electronic, mechanical, photocopying, recording or otherwise), without the prior written permission of both the copyright owner and the above publisher of this book.

British Library Cataloguing-in-Publication Data
A catalogue record for this book is available from the British Library.

Library of Congress Control Number: 2022949712
Names: Braber, Ben, author.
Title: Individuals and small groups in Jewish resistance to the Holocaust : a case study of a young couple and their friends / Ben Braber.
Description: London ; New York, NY : Anthem Press, [2022] | Includes bibliographical references and index. |
Identifiers: LCCN 2022949712 | ISBN 9781839988288 (paperback) | ISBN 9781839983603 (epub) | ISBN 9781839983597 (pdf)
Subjects: LCSH: Bueno de Mesquita, Nol, 1908–2002. | Kolthoff, Ter, 1913–1990. | World War, 1939–1945–Jewish resistance–Netherlands. | Holocaust, Jewish (1939–1945)–Netherlands. | Jews–Netherlands–Biography. | World War, 1939–1945–Jewish resistance–Netherlands–Historiography.
Classification: LCC DS135.N6 B725 | DDC 940.53/183209492–dc23/eng/20220119
LC record available at https://lccn.loc.gov/2022949712

ISBN-13: 978-1-83998-828-8 (Pbk)
ISBN-10: 1-83998-828-2 (Pbk)

Cover image: Ter Kolthoff and Nol Bueno de Mesquita (photographer unknown)

This title is also available as an e-book.

CONTENTS

Illustrations   vii
Preface to the 2023 Edition   ix
Prologue   xi

Introduction   1
1. Mokum and Mediene   11
2. The Wedding   19
3. The Rising Tide   35
4. The Birth of Ruth   53
5. Deportation   61
6. Escape from Westerbork   83
7. The Birth of Marjan   97
8. Murder in the Gallery   101
9. In Hiding   113
Epilogue   121
Conclusion   125

Sources and Bibliography   135
Index   145

ILLUSTRATIONS

Front cover Ter Kolthoff and Nol Bueno de Mesquita

1	Nol Bueno de Mesquita in 1985	xii
2	Map of the Netherlands	12
3	Map of Amsterdam	15
4	Advert for Nol's Interior Design Business	21
5	Map of the Waterloo Square	42
6	Map of Westerbork	84
7	Hedwig and Jupp Mahler	94
8	*Das Gefesselte Theater*	116

PREFACE TO THE 2023 EDITION

After the publication of the hardback of this book in 2022, I have been asked several times: How much Jewish resistance was there in the Netherlands during the years of German occupation (1940–1945); how many people were involved? The answer is that we don't know exactly.

However, since 1961 we have an idea. In that year the historian Jacques Presser published his thesis, claiming that (1) Jewish resistance in the Netherlands was as much overestimated by the German occupiers of the country as it was underrated by the Dutch and that (2) resistance by Jews in the Netherlands had relatively exceeded resistance by non-Jews.[1] He based his thesis on the Roll of Honour, a list of fallen soldiers and resistance members. Presser had identified large numbers of names on this list as Jewish. He also found hundreds of names of Jewish resistance members in the documents he examined during his research for his work on the persecution and destruction of Dutch Jewry between 1940 and 1945 – *Ondergang* (1965), which he compared to what was known at the time about numbers of general resistance members.[2] Presser didn't mention exact figures but based on his thesis the following calculation can be made.

During the last pre-war census, over 111,000 Jews were in the Netherlands in 1930. They formed 1.41 per cent of the total Dutch population of 7.83 million. In 1941 about 140,000 Jews were registered in the Netherlands according to Nazi yardsticks (representing 1.56 per cent of the total population, which had grown to 8.92 million).[3]

According to the historian Loe de Jong, in his work *Het Koninkrijk der Nederlanden in de Tweede Wereldoorlog* (1976), an estimated 45,000 illegal workers were active in the Netherlands during the entire period of German occupation between 1940 and 1945. This corresponds with a half per cent of the

---

1. The thesis was published in 1961 in a newspaper article in *Het Vaderland*, reprinted the same year in Presser, *Schrijfsels en Schrifturen*, 138–146.
2. Presser, *Ondergang*, vol. II, 7.
3. For details on the Jewish population, see chapter 1; for the figures on the total Dutch population, see https://www.cbs.nl.

total population. De Jong defined an illegal worker as somebody who was active clandestinely as an individual or member of organised collectives in their resistance to the German occupiers.[4]

In 1990, I mentioned over a thousand names of Jewish illegal workers in my book *Zelfs als wij zullen verliezen*. That's more than two-thirds of a percentage of the Jewish population in the registration of 1941, which confirms the second part of Presser's thesis.

The figure of a thousand illegal Jewish workers I mentioned in 1990 is a low estimate. Since then, more research has been conducted, which has brought to light the resistance activity of numerous, but until then unknown, Jewish resistance members.

However, it's presently still impossible to give an exact number of Jews involved in resistance. Does that matter? I don't think so. Figures are important, but to gain greater knowledge about Jewish life during the Holocaust and get a deeper understanding of Jewish resistance we can also look at personal circumstances and characteristics of Jewish resistance members and the formation of small Jewish resistance groups. And that's what I've done in this book.

---

4. De Jong, *Het Koninkrijk der Nederlanden in de Tweede Wereldoorlog*, vol. VII, 1029–1090.

PROLOGUE

He raced up the stairs. Blond curls messy as always. The grooves in his otherwise young face had long been deep, but now Krijn Breur looked extremely worried. And agitated. Bursting into the first floor flat, he shouted: 'Nol, you need to get out of here. At once. We've been betrayed.'[1] That last word wasn't lost on Nol Bueno de Mesquita. A bit older, wearing spectacles and with wavy dark hair, Nol had always feared betrayal, but it took time to grasp the first part of Krijn's message. Get out, yes. But how?

Two and a half years earlier German armies had occupied the Netherlands, where Nol had married Ter Kolthoff in June 1940, barely a month after the invasion. When a friend had asked the Jewish couple that summer to 'do something against these rotters',[2] they had joined resistance groups. The consequences of that step overtook them in 1942. The German police and their Dutch helpers were hunting Krijn and his fellow resistance fighters. The trail led to Nol and Ter's flat on an Amsterdam canal, just outside the old Jewish neighbourhood. Their daughter Ruth was only one and a half years old and Ter suspected being pregnant again. It was getting cold; the winter frost was about to descend. Days were shortening. The evening curfew made it dangerous to go out at night. Actually, it was just as unsafe in daylight. There were roadblocks, raids and round ups. The deportation of Jews from the Netherlands was in full swing. Was it possible to escape? And if so, where could they go?

They got away, because I met Nol in 1985, 40 years after the end of the Second World War. Although ageing and balding, he strongly resembled the man he had been in 1942. As he told me his story, Nol was serious, but occasionally his eyes betrayed a streak of mischief.

The reason for meeting Nol was to ask him about his wartime experience. At the time I was studying history at the University of Amsterdam, following

---

1. Interview A. Bueno de Mesquita.
2. Interview A. Bueno de Mesquita.

Illustration 1. Nol Bueno de Mesquita in 1985 (photo Norma Braber-McKinney).

a few years of journalistic work, and I earned a living for my young family by working as a freelance reporter. This work took me to Nol.

In February 1983, the German war criminal Klaus Barbie had been flown from Bolivia to stand trial in France, where during the Second World War the *Hauptsturmführer* of the *Schutzstaffel* (SS) had become notorious as the 'Butcher of Lyons'. I discovered that Barbie had been posted in Amsterdam before he gained notoriety in Lyons. It emerged that before May 1940 the German police had been spying on political opponents who had fled to the Netherlands. Some refugees had been arrested as the Germans occupied Dutch soil. Barbie seemed to have been involved and may have conducted their interrogation. I decided to speak to survivors. The accounts they gave provided useful information about Barbie, but some also contained an extraordinary revelation – a so far untold story of a resistance group consisting almost entirely of Jews that had operated in the Netherlands, helping people to escape from deportation centres and concentration camps.

Jewish resistance was often overlooked. In the 1980s, when people thought about the Holocaust, they usually imagined Jews as victims. This image was correct. In the Holocaust 71 per cent of Dutch Jewry perished; of the about

140,000 Jews in the Netherlands just over 100,000 were murdered by the National Socialists. When Amsterdam was liberated in 1945, only about 5,000 of the more than 65,000 Jews who had lived in the capital of the Netherlands five years earlier were still alive in the city. That loss of life was proportionally higher than in other Western European countries.[3] It helped to give rise to the long-lived myth that the Jews were led as lambs to the slaughter.[4] A photo[5] of a group of people reporting for deportation in Amsterdam in 1943 seems to support that widespread view. The foreground shows a family – mum, dad and a child. With them walks an elderly man, possibly the child's grandad. They lug heavy suitcases, bags and rucksacks. All are dressed in their Sunday-best. It's summer, but they wear heavy overcoats. There's a star on their outer clothing. They appear docile, being led as lambs. However, this perception was contradicted by the refugee accounts I heard, which emphasised Jewish attempts to resist the persecution.

Following that finding, between 1983 and 1987, I conducted a further series of interviews with members of resistance groups and eyewitnesses. That's how I got to visit Nol. He and others gave me more remarkable details, and I searched archives for documentary support of their statements. I also contacted people who had known or knew about individual members of Nol's group. All this material found its way into my 1985 graduation thesis.[6] A journalistic version of this thesis was published in 1987,[7] followed in 1990 by a more comprehensive study on Jewish resistance in the Netherlands,[8] which went some way towards correcting the public perception of Jews in the Holocaust.

---

3. Vital, *A People Apart*, 897; Hess, 'Disproportionate Destruction'; Hirschfeld, 'Niederlande'. Compare Croes, 'The Holocaust in the Netherlands and the Rate of Jewish Survival'. For more details and overviews of Jews in the Netherlands under German occupation: Barnouw, *Geschiedenis van Nederland 1940–1945*; Blom, 'Nederland onder Duitse bezetting 10 mei 1940–5 mei 1945'; Blom, 'The Persecution of the Jews in the Netherlands'; Herzberg, *Kroniek der Jodenvervolging, 1940–1945*; Houwink ten Cate, '"Het Jongere Deel"'; De Jong, *Het Koninkrijk der Nederlanden in de Tweede Wereldoorlog*, vol. VIII; Michman, Beem, Michman, *Pinkas*; Presser, *Ondergang*; Romijn, 'The Experience of the Jews in the Netherlands during the German Occupation'; Romijn,'The War, 1940–1945'; Romijn, Boom, Griffioen, Zeller, Meeuwenoord, Houwink Ten Cate, *The Persecution of the Jews in the Netherlands, 1940–1945*.
4. See for example, *De Telegraaf* 8 June 2019.
5. NIOD Beeldbank WO2: 96771: deportation of Jews from Amsterdam 20 June 1943 (http://www.beeldbankwo2).
6. Braber, 'Passage naar vrijheid' (1985).
7. Braber, *Passage naar vrijheid* (1987).
8. Braber, *Zelfs als wij zullen verliezen*.

Although I didn't meet Nol again, he'd from time to time pop up in my head. Such an occasion occurred 30 years after the interview and 13 years after he died.

In the meantime, my interest as a historian had been broadened to issues surrounding integration of immigrants and their descendants into Western European societies after 1800. Jews had been among these immigrants and I attempted to understand Jewish resistance within an integration framework, as it offered an example of how a group that was integrating responded to being segregated by force. This resulted in my 2013 monograph *This Cannot Happen Here: Integration and Jewish Resistance in the Netherlands, 1940–1945* (published in the series Studies of the NIOD Institute for War, Holocaust and Genocide Studies).

Looking for patterns and exceptions, I examined the setting in which Jewish resistance had occurred in the Netherlands and made brief comparisons to events and developments in Germany, Italy, Belgium and France. This review found that the manner of integration of Jews into the Dutch society as well as the speed and direction of that process had influenced their resistance during the Holocaust. However, it also concluded that we actually still knew very little about Jewish resistance and that our understanding could only be deepened by shedding more light on individual Jewish resistance members.[9] Following that conclusion, I returned to Nol's story, understood the role his wife Ter had played and published a Dutch book on their experiences.[10]

That book – a tale of life, love and loss – was launched in Amsterdam in 2015. Nol's mischievous look came to my mind when people spoke about him during the launch. After that event, the image returns every time someone mentions him. It makes me realise now that when I met Nol, I learned a precious lesson about human behaviour, which was later validated in my studies and changed the way I view history. That lesson enlightens this book.

---

9. Braber, *This Cannot Happen Here*, 155–65.
10. Braber, *Waren mijn ogen een bron van tranen*.

INTRODUCTION

This book aims to increase our knowledge and deepen the understanding of Jewish resistance to the Holocaust by examining personal circumstances and characteristics of Jewish resistance members and the formation of small Jewish resistance groups. It treats the term 'Jewish resistance' the same as 'resistance by Jews' and 'participation of Jews in resistance'. To determine who can be regarded as a Jew, this book uses a description formulated by Alderman, who has defined as Jewish any person who considered or considers themselves to be Jewish, or who was or is regarded as such by their contemporaries.[1] What consists of resistance is discussed below.

A long historiography of Jewish resistance precedes this book, stretching back to the first years after the Second World War. The scope of this book doesn't allow a review of that vast and evolving body of work or to mention all pioneering authors.[2] Instead, a selection is made of writers who have provided broad and inclusive definitions of Jewish resistance, which are applied in this book, or who have offered new outlooks on Jewish resistance in Western Europe, such as attention for integration and gender issues, which also figure here, or who have dealt with Jewish resistance in the Netherlands, where the couple in the subtitle of this book lived.

Dinur and Friedman have been early proponents of a broad definition of Jewish resistance.[3] Robinson, Suhl and Steinberg have also formulated such descriptions,[4] which were further discussed after the 1968 Yad Vashem

---

1. Alderman, *Modern British Jewry*, 1–2. Compare Schöffer, 'Introduction', 11.
2. Stone, 'Introduction'. See also Stone, *History, Memory and Mass Atrocity*, vii, x, 246–7. For a comprehensive review of the historiography see Rozett, 'Jewish Resistance'; Bloxham, Kushner, *The Holocaust*.
3. Dinur, 'Problems Confronting "Yad Vashem" in its Work of Research'; Friedman, 'Preliminary and Methodological Problems of the Research on the Jewish Catastrophe in the Nazi Period'. I'm grateful to the late Conny Kristel (*Geschiedschrijving als opdracht*, 119–20, 125), who has pointed me in this direction.
4. Robinson, 'Concluding Remarks'; Suhl, *They Fought Back*; Steinberg, *La Révolte des justes*.

conference on Jewish resistance.[5] One of the historians who have more recently coined definitions of Jewish resistance is Bauer, who has described Jewish resistance as group or individual actions consciously taken by Jews in opposition to known or surmised laws, actions or intentions directed against the Jews by the National Socialists and their supporters.[6]

Michman and Marrus have shown how this resistance incorporated various forms and was conducted on different levels. Michman has argued that Jewish resistance encompassed three broad categories: armed, conscious and committed resistance, such as ghetto uprisings; non-violent resistance that was active, organised, committed and conscious, such as rescue efforts; and non-violent resistance that was unorganised and intuitive, such as self-preservation and the sanctification of life.[7]

Using a model of general resistance presented by Rings,[8] Marrus has suggested the application of a more detailed classification. It includes symbolic, polemic, defensive, offensive and enchained resistance. In these categories, symbolic resistance consists of gestures and expressions, such as spiritual acts and the sanctification of life, which showed that people refused to be terrorised and remained committed to their religion or culture. Polemic resistance goes further as people raised their voice in protest, usually at great risk to themselves, for example, through public statements and clandestine publications. This category also covers going into hiding to conduct this type of resistance. Defensive resistance is giving aid to others and the defence of lives and values by individuals and groups, initially through permitted activity but increasingly through clandestine work. Offensive resistance consists of armed acts. Jewish participation in general (i.e. not specifically Jewish) resistance falls in the polemic, defensive and offensive resistance categories. In contrast, enchained resistance is the desperate fight of those Jews who were cut off, for example, in ghettos and camps, to defend their honour or fight for the future, without help and practically no hope of survival.[9]

---

5. Dawidowicz, *The War against the Jews, 1933–1945*; Kohn, Grubstein, *Jewish Resistance During the Holocaust*; Michel, 'Jewish Resistance and the European Resistance Movement'; Trunk, *Jewish Responses to Nazi Persecution*.
6. Bauer, *They Chose Life*; Bauer, *The Jewish Emergence from Powerlessness*; Bauer, *Rethinking the Holocaust*.
7. Michman, *Holocaust Historiography*, 217–48.
8. Rings, *Life with the Enemy*.
9. Marrus, 'Varieties of Jewish Resistance'; Marrus, 'Jewish Resistance to the Holocaust'.

INTRODUCTION

Using these definitions and categories, historians have explored resistance within the totality of Jewish life under the National Socialists.[10] Comparative studies have also given insights into the ways in which different forms of Jewish resistance developed. For example, as Moore[11] has indicated, Jewish rescue and aid efforts across Western Europe could only succeed with non-Jewish assistance, which was, among other factors, influenced by pre-war relationships between Jewish communities and non-Jewish populations. Others, including Poznanski[12] and Rohrlich[13], have reviewed Jewish resistance within the framework of integration of Jews into the societies of the countries in which they lived or examined specific issues, such as gender.

Jewish resistance has been a somewhat neglected topic in Dutch historiography. However, there have been exceptions. De Wolff and Wielek have broached the subject briefly in their wider studies of Jews in the Netherlands during the period of German occupation.[14] Herzberg and Presser have emulated them.[15] De Jong has discussed Jewish resistance in his multi-volume study of the history of the Netherlands during the Second World War.[16]

Herzberg has concluded that there were no opportunities for armed or organised resistance for Dutch Jews during the war. Instead, he has highlighted reactions to the persecution, such as the spiritual mobilisation, flourishing of Jewish cultural life and return of many to Judaism.[17] Utilising the work of Dinur and Friedman, Presser has asserted that: 1. the resistance of Jews in the Netherlands during the Second World War was as much overestimated by the Germans as the Dutch underestimated it; and 2. the resistance of Jews in the Netherlands relatively exceeded that of non-Jews. He has also listed various instances of resistance, conducted by individuals and groups.[18]

---

10. See, for example, Friedländer, *Nazi Germany and the Jews, Volume 1: The Years of Persecution, 1933–1939*, and *Volume 2: The Years of Extermination, 1939–1945*; Glass, *Jewish Resistance During the Holocaust*; Kaplan, *Between Dignity and Despair*; Lazare, *Rescue as Resistance*; Stone, *History, Memory and Mass Atrocity*; Tec, *Jewish Resistance*; Tzur, 'Resistance in Western Europe'; Yahil, *The Holocaust*.
11. Moore, 'The Rescue of Jews from Nazi Persecution'.
12. Poznanski, 'A Methodological Approach to the Study of Jewish Resistance in France'; Poznanski, 'Anti-Semitism and the Rescue of Jews in France.'; Poznanski, *Jews in France during World War II*.
13. Rohrlich, *Resisting the Holocaust*.
14. Wielek, *De oorlog die Hitler won*; De Wolff, *Geschiedenis der joden in Nederland*.
15. Herzberg, *Kroniek der Jodenvervolging, 1940–1945*; Presser, *Ondergang*.
16. De Jong, *Het Koninkrijk der Nederlanden in de Tweede Wereldoorlog*.
17. Herzberg, *Kroniek der Jodenvervolging, 1940–1945*, 226–30.
18. Presser, *Ondergang*, vol. II, 3–18.

On par with Bauer, De Jong has defined wartime resistance in the Netherlands in general as every action taken by people to prevent the National Socialist occupiers from realising their objectives.[19] As will be discussed later, this definition echoes what Lodewijk Visser wrote during the war. Like Herzberg, De Jong has found that armed resistance against the deportations was impossible, but he has argued that this doesn't imply a general passive attitude among Jews and he has regularly pointed at the large numbers of Jews who ignored the summons for deportation and went into hiding.[20] Unlike Herzberg and Presser, De Jong hasn't discussed spiritual resistance. Instead, throughout his work De Jong has described the participation of Jews in the general resistance as well as the background and activity of individuals.

During the 1980s and early 1990s Herzberg, Presser and De Jong were followed by a range of authors who published research on specific individuals, groups and locations. For example, Avni, Brasz, Daams, Ofek, Keny and Pinkhof, and Regenhardt and Groot have reconstructed the activity of young Zionists, while Van de Kar has related his own resistance work as well as the activity of others who rescued Jewish children, and these rescuers have also been the subjects of works by Roegholt and Wiedeman and Schellekens.[21] And I followed my study of one group with a more comprehensive work, which also investigated Presser's assertions.[22] However, after the publications of the early 1990s, the attention for Jewish resistance ebbed away in the Netherlands.[23]

The first aim of my 2013 study *This Cannot Happen Here* was to apply a broad and inclusive definition of Jewish resistance, notably the classifications

---

19. De Jong, *Het Koninkrijk der Nederlanden in de Tweede Wereldoorlog*, vol. VII, 1029.
20. De Jong, *Het Koninkrijk der Nederlanden in de Tweede Wereldoorlog*, vol. VIII deals with the persecution of the Jews.
21. Avni, 'Zionist Underground in Holland and France and the Escape to Spain'; Brasz, Daams Czn, Ofek, Keny, Pinkhof, *De jeugdalijah van het Paviljoen Loosdrechtse Rade 1939–1945*; Van de Kar, *Joods Verzet*; Regenhardt, Groot, *Om nooit te vergeten*; Roegholt, Wiedeman, *Walter Suskind and a Theatre in Holland*; Schellekens, 'Op zoek naar Walter Süskind'. See also Cohen, Cochavi, *Studies on the Shoah*.
22. Braber, *Passage naar vrijheid*; Braber, *Zelfs als wij zullen verliezen*.
23. Notable exceptions were Michman, *Holocaust Historiography*; Moore, *Survivors*; Moore, *Victims and Survivors*; Romijn, 'The War, 1940–1945'. Moore has offered an understanding of why and how Jews in different countries developed strategies for survival in terms of rescue and aid work, but he didn't deal with other forms of resistance. The first two studies were not solely dedicated to the Netherlands. The last two works have incorporated the existing literature on Jewish resistance but did not provide new views on this topic. Other works related to this subject that appeared before 2013 include, in chronological order: Eman, *Things We Couldn't Say*; Bolle, *Ben's Story*; Flim, *Saving the Children*; Klempner, *The Heart Has Reasons*.

provided by Michman and Marrus, to review this resistance in the Netherlands within a framework of integration of Jews into Dutch society. My second objective was to encourage new research and reignite the debate about Jewish resistance. I did occasionally find a clear link between integration and resistance. This connection directly influenced the actions of some rabbis and individuals outside the religious leadership. The social position of Jews also lay behind many public protests uttered by them. And it moulded the ways in which Jews participated in general resistance organisations. However, integration not always affected the manner in which Jews conducted armed resistance in the Netherlands. It assisted as well as hindered people going into hiding and had different effects on Jewish rescue and aid work, which was often conducted by people who were not well integrated but couldn't succeed without the help of non-Jews or well-integrated Jews. Often so many and sometimes contradicting issues determined a form of Jewish resistance that it's impossible to emphasise one factor. Personal motives, individual characteristics and local circumstances influenced resistance too, but as the conclusion of *This Cannot Happen Here* stated, when that book was published, we still knew little about most participants in Jewish resistance.[24]

Following that book, and partly because of its publication, other researchers, scholars, journalists and other writers have unearthed and used biographical information on Jewish resistance members in the Netherlands, focussing on particular individuals, families, groups and activities. They include, to mention just a few authors in the chronological order in which their work appeared, Wasserstein, Schippers, Van Tongeren, Admiraal, Veldman and Schwegman, Bar-Efrat, Tallentire, Van Iperen, Geerlings, Katan and Sanders.[25] A recently published family history collection has added portraits of some 40 individual Jews in resistance in the Netherlands.[26] Furthermore, other sources have become available in digital format, for example, the website *Joods Amsterdam*,[27] which contains descriptions of places and people in the Dutch capital, including Jewish resistance members.

Internationally our knowledge and understanding of Jewish resistance has been widened and deepened too. For example, through monographs written

---

24. Braber, *This Cannot Happen Here*, 163.
25. Wasserstein, *The Ambiguity or Virtue*; Schippers, *De Westerweelgroep en de Palestinapioniers*; Van Tongeren, Admiraal, Veldman, Schwegman, *Jacoba van Tongeren en de onbekende verzetshelden van Groep 2000 (1940–1945)*; Bar-Efrat, *Denunciation and Rescue*; Tallentire, *Leo*; Van Iperen, *'t Hooge Nest*; Geerlings, 'Survivor, Agitator'; Katan, *Geen makke schepen*; Sanders, *Adje Cohen*.
26. Sprenger, *Gezichten van Joods verzet*.
27. https://www.joodsamsterdam.nl.

and collections edited by Land-Weber, Rappaport, Gutterman, Henry, Michman, Paldiel, Roland, and Tydor Baumel-Schwartz and Schneider.[28]

Occasionally, the new literature on individuals and families seems intended to show that some Jews were more courageous than other Jews and therefore resisted the persecution. However, how do you measure courage? Were persons who took up arms braver than parents who decided to stay with their children and be deported together when there were not enough places to hide? This book can, of course, not answer these questions. Instead, it responds to what Tydor Baumel-Schwarz has asked in her introduction[29] to the collection *All Our Brothers and Sisters*, which can be summarised as: Did Jews who saved other Jews during the Holocaust embody specific characteristics and personalities or share certain identities and worldviews? For that purpose, this book describes and analyses the factors which triggered the resistance of individuals and small groups and shaped their resistance. That review thus considers the causes for people to resist, the moment and manner they chose to act and the results of these choices, what influenced their decisions and subsequent resistance work, and who took initiatives and drew in others. It reveals how, next to social processes and remarkable personalities, unpredictable coincidence and ordinary people changed the dynamics and course and of history.

As a result, this book differs from *This Cannot Happen Here*. My 2013 publication and the book you're reading now have the same overall subject: Jewish resistance, and there's some unavoidable overlap in contents. Nevertheless, the two books are different. In 2013, I examined the subject within the framework of the integration of Jews into Dutch society, reviewing population groups and group behaviour. This book, however, deals with individuals and their actions, with detailed descriptions of personal characteristics and circumstances that resulted in the formation of small Jewish resistance groups. It closely follows a couple and their friends in their resistance during the Holocaust. It also incorporates evidence that has come to light following the 2013 publication.

This book is not a comprehensive report on all forms of Jewish resistance in the Netherlands or a register of everybody who was involved in that activity. It touches on various forms of Jewish resistance and the participation of Jews in general resistance, but it's impossible to name all the involved individuals and groups. The central characters in this story are Nol Bueno de Mesquita, Ter Kolthoff and some of their friends. These persons have been chosen because

---

28. Land-Weber, *To Save a Life*; Rappaport, *Beyond Courage*; Gutterman, *Fighting For Her People*; Henry, *Jewish Resistance Against the Nazis*; Michman, *Hiding, Sheltering, and Borrowing Identities*; Paldiel, *Saving One's Own;* Roland, *The Jewish Resistance*; Tydor Baumel-Schwartz, Schneider, *All Our Brothers and Sisters*.
29. Tydor Baumel-Schwartz, 'Introduction', 19–24.

they were connected to and active in several forms of Jewish resistance or played a key role in one of more of its manifestations.

The information for this study comes from various sources. I had the honour to speak to Jews who resisted the German occupation of the Netherlands and the persecution of Jews. During the 1980s I interviewed Nol, Ter and others. Parts of these interviews have been published in edited versions and were followed by other publications, but for this book I've used what the interviewees originally told me. For example, following my interview in 1985, Nol wrote two books, one about the Sephardic Jews of Amsterdam and the other containing his memories of working as an interior designer. The Jewish Historical Museum in Amsterdam also has a recorded interview with Nol, while his professional work archives have been preserved in the New Institute in Rotterdam. I'm aware of this material, but for this book I rely on what Nol told me. I'm grateful to him and the other people who spoke to me, and I hope to have made good use of the privilege they granted me by telling their story.

One of the things that struck me during the 1980s interviews was that until then most interviewees had never talked about their wartime experience. For example, Ter lived in Amsterdam-North, just like me, and I had known her for years, but she had never mentioned her resistance activity or told other people I knew. One reason for that silence was, according to one of Ter's friends: 'It was hidden too deep [...] Everybody kept it hidden.'[30] In other words, the subject was too painful to discuss.

Perhaps Ter's friend was right, but later I discovered that three years before my interview, Ter had spoken on one occasion in public about one of her wartime experiences, namely that of being a mother. That instance had been recorded and parts of the recording were incorporated in a television documentary about Dutch women during the German occupation of the Netherlands. It was broadcast in 1980. In this documentary, Ter related what had happened to her daughters Ruth and Marjan, which she repeated almost word-by-word to me.

There's a special reason for relying on what the interviewees originally told me. Oral history has potential pitfalls, notably the subjectivity of interviewees, the way they remember and the influence of traumas they suffered; memory and recall are fragile.[31] This is caused by physical and mental processes. For most

---

30. Interview T. van Reemst-De Vries.
31. There is an extensive literature on this subject. For example, Abrams, *Oral History Theory*; Ankersmit, *Historical Representation*; O'Keane, *The Rag and Bone Shop*; Sacks, *The Man Who Mistook His Wife for a Hat and Other Clinical Tales*; Thompson, *The Voice of the Past*.

people, as they experience events and recollect the past in their mind, memories are formed by connections in the brain. They create a wide but irregular network. In this uneven grid a passing experience turns into an enduring record, with associated emotions and sensations, such as images, smells and sounds. These records can be hidden deeply, for example, as a result of trauma, but they come to life every time they're remembered. However, the contents of the records can change each time they're recalled. When people remember an event, they usually evoke the last memory of that event. Or the last time they told somebody what they recall. As time passes or health deteriorates, memories lose their realistic and cinematic quality and become fuzzier, more like fading snapshots. New events or stimuli can refocus these mental images, but they usually leave their own mark. Furthermore, in their memory people can construct stories that satisfy a need to provide a coherent narrative. The way in which we remember the past – and give it meaning – helps us to make sense of the present; providing yet another way in which today influences recollection of yesterday. All this affects the historical truthfulness of memories, possibly diminishing the reliability of oral history evidence.

However, while memories can change every time they are retold, the brain retains the original sensation or mental image associated with an event, which can be recalled in an oral history interview. For that purpose, I used a method of asking the interviewees to tell me their whole life story; carefully listening and only at appropriate moments raising open questions to help them recall what they felt during an event they are relating, which was aimed to bring out the original memory of that event. Furthermore, I was able to locate in numerous archive collections supporting evidence for the stories I was told. I also contacted people who had known or knew about individual resistance members. Finally, I used the existing literature and other sources of information, such as digital databanks and websites, including *Oorlogsbronnen*[32] which offers access to multiple records of the Netherlands during the Second World War.

The result is a case study that brings it all together, examines primary and secondary sources and uses a qualitative analysis to investigate individual and small group manifestations of Jewish resistance during the German occupation of the Netherlands between 1940 and 1945. This study contributes to the historiography, but its focus enables an interpretation that displays a distinctive view of history.

Some final words about the structure of this book. Following the preface, prologue and introduction, the first chapter contains a brief description of the Netherlands and its Jewish population on the eve of the Second World War.

---

32. https://www.oorlogsbronnen.nl.

The subsequent eight chapters first introduce Nol and Ter and their friends and then tell their story in a largely chronological order. The epilogue relates what happened after the war. Each chapter finishes with a summary of the presented information. These summaries underpin the general conclusions drawn at the end of this book, before it closes with a list of sources, bibliography and index.

Chapter 1

MOKUM AND MEDIENE

It's easy to stand out in a flat country. And when that country is small and you've been noticed, hiding is hard. So, where could Ter and Nol go after they found the police on their trail in 1942?

On the eve of the Second World War, less than nine million people inhabited the Kingdom of the Netherlands on the western outskirts of the European continent, where the Rhine, Meuse and Scheldt flow into the North Sea. About a quarter of the land fell below sea level. Large stretches in the north and west had been reclaimed from river estuaries and sea inlets. They were surrounded with dykes and, despite occasional floods, protected by an ingenious polder system powered by windmills, steam engines and electrical pumps. Agriculture, notably cattle breeding and milk farming, dominated the green landscape, where countless rivers, canals and ditches cut through the soggy soil. Foremost among numerous lakes was the IJsselmeer that had been created in 1932 by the completion of a dam with a length of 32 kilometres between the provinces of North Holland and Friesland to separate the South Sea from the North Sea. The horizon was broken up by church steeples in towns and villages. Much of the urban wealth was founded on trade, including a share of the transatlantic slave trade, and exploitation of colonies, involving the subjection of their native population and application of slave labour.

For centuries Jews had lived in the Netherlands, and by 1939 they were becoming an integrated yet still distinctive part of Dutch society. In 1930, at the last official population count before the outbreak of war, 111,917 persons were registered as a member of a Jewish religious congregation. That was a comparatively small group, forming just over 1 per cent of the total Dutch population. In addition, at the time of the census on 31 December 1930 there were about 30,000 persons who weren't officially counted as Jews because they didn't belong to a Jewish congregation, but who can be regarded as Jews. The Jews formed a declining population segment. In 1920 the census had counted 115,223 Jews – about 3,000 more than in 1930. Furthermore, it was a quickly

Illustration 2. In 1940 the Netherlands covered less than 40,000 square kilometres. A small country; as the crow flies, the distance between Groningen in the north and Maastricht in the south is 270 kilometres, between The Hague in the west and Enschede in the east it's 176 kilometres. In 1937 the Netherlands had an area in size roughly one-sixth of the United Kingdom, one-eleventh of Germany and one-fourteenth of France; miniscule compared to the United States and Soviet Union.

ageing group with fewer children than other population segments.¹ In addition, by 1939 about 14,500 Jews from Germany lived in the Netherlands, of which 85 per cent had arrived after Hitler's rise to power in 1933. Next to the German-Jewish refugees fleeing the National Socialist persecution there were about 3,000 foreign Jews who had become stateless. Half of the total number of refugees resided in Amsterdam. They were pitied, but during the 1930s their presence had increasingly been perceived as unwanted by the Dutch authorities. There was also tension between Dutch and German Jews. Many of the first group felt the German Jews had brought persecution upon themselves.²

Dutch Jewry was concentrated in a few areas of the Netherlands and urbanisation among them was more extensive than among non-Jews. In 1930, about 80 per cent of all Jews in the Netherlands lived in the two western provinces of North and South Holland. The remainder was divided over the other ten provinces. They were mainly city dwellers; only one-fifth of Dutch Jewry lived in villages or towns with less than 100,000 inhabitants. The Netherlands had few large cities. Amsterdam, the country's capital, located in the province of North Holland, had about 700,000 residents. The city, often denoted with the Yiddish word *Mokum* (from the Hebrew *makom* – place*)*, was the main centre of Jewish residence; 58 per cent of all the Jews in the Netherlands lived there (in contrast, just under 10 per cent of the total Dutch population was concentrated in the capital). In Amsterdam, the just over 65,000 Jews living there represented a substantial population segment. However, here their number was also declining – it decreased by more than 3,000 in the years between 1920 and 1930 – and the Jewish share of the city's population dropped from 12 to 9 per cent. Outside the capital, in what Jews called the *Mediene* (country*)*, several towns had sizeable Jewish populations. Rotterdam and The Hague, both in the province of South Holland, each had about 10,000 Jewish inhabitants. Groningen in the north of the country had about 2,000 Jewish residents and Utrecht, Apeldoorn and Arnhem in the centre and east had about 1,000 each.

Amsterdam, connected via a canal completed in 1876 to the North Sea at IJmuiden, north of Haarlem, displayed the hustle and bustle of a busy harbour, based on colonial wares from Asia, the Caribbean and Latin America, but also with new industries such as aviation, including the Fokker

---

1. Cohen, 'Boekman's Legacy'; Gans, *Memorboek*, 831, De Jong, *Het Koninkrijk der Nederlanden in de Tweede Wereldoorlog*, vol. IV, 874–5, vol. V, 496; Kruijt, 'Het Jodendom in de Nederlandse samenleving'; Presser, *Ondergang*, vol. I, 54–78, 96–7, 401–18, 420; Schöffer, 'Nederland en de joden in de jaren dertig in historisch perspectief', 88–90; Sijes, *Studies*, 128.
2. Presser, *Ondergang*, vol. I, 417–22.

factory. It was the capital of a changing country. The Dutch economy was becoming part of a wider Western European entity. The foundations were laid of what were to become global corporations, such as Philips, Shell and Unilever. The port of Rotterdam started to thrive. Closer cultural contacts were cemented with other countries. New international artistic and political movements found supporters in the Netherlands. Religious minorities, working class people and women were further integrated into the Dutch society. The population of fast-growing cities often professed a get-up-and-go and can-do mentality, to which immigrants such as the Jews contributed extensively. Amsterdam was bursting at its seams with the constant arrival of new migrants. More and more young residents were leaving the centre of the capital, moving to new-built suburbs, but newcomers instantly took places vacated in the old city.

The Jewish quarter of Amsterdam lingered at the eastern end of the city centre, with its concentric belts of canals that had been dug during the Dutch Golden Age. The Jewish neighbourhood stretched from the Waterloo Square next to the river Amstel, which gave the city its name, to the New Market and Old Sconce near the IJ, an inlet of the South Sea that had originally made Amsterdam an international port. At a brisk pace, you could walk in less than a quarter of an hour along the western rim of the Jewish quarter. Parallel to the edge ran a series of long but narrow streets. There, and in smaller side streets and back alleys, Jews were not the sole inhabitants of the neighbourhood – they shared with non-Jews the overcrowded and dilapidated tenements, often four floors high.

Nor did Jews exclusively live in the Jewish quarter, they resided all over the city but clustered in some areas. If you crossed the stately Nieuwe Herengracht, an eastward extension of the second of the city's main circular canals, you entered the Plantation District, a neighbourhood for the better-off. Jews who could afford homes in a sought-after area also lived in Plan South, near the sport stadium that had been built for the 1928 Olympic Games. Working class Jews dwelled in the old neighbourhood and further north and east in housing estates erected to accommodate people who were evicted from city centre slums when large-scale demolition started in earnest. The Weesp Street bordered the west side of the Plantation District. In the poor patches of this area Polish Jews had taken refuge. Crossing the Amstel took you to the Frederik Square, the location of the formerly imposing Palace of People's Industry, erected to mimic international exhibition buildings in London and Paris. A spectacular fire in 1929 had destroyed the Palace's glass dome, but the adjacent Gallery, a covered shopping passage, had escaped the inferno. From there you could walk into the Utrecht Street, to the Rembrandt Square, over the Blue Bridge across the Amstel and back into the Waterloo Square. On

Illustration 3. In 1941 the municipality of Amsterdam produced a map that registered the number of Jews living in the city. A dot represents ten Jews. The darker areas are neighbourhoods with relatively many Jews.

market days, people from all over Amsterdam flocked to the quarter to see Jewish stallholders at work.

Jews had long been excluded from areas of Dutch social, economic and political life, but at the end of the eighteenth century they had received civil rights equal to the rest of the population and their integration into the wider society had begun.[3] During the integration process, the Jewish group became

---

3. For overviews of Jewish life in the Netherlands and integration before 1940 see: Blom, 'Dutch Jews, Jewish Dutchmen and Jews in the Netherlands'; Blom, Cahen, 'Jewish Netherlanders, Netherlands Jews, and Jews in the Netherlands, 1870–1940'; Braber, *This Cannot Happen Here*, 17–80; Daalder, 'Dutch Jews in a Segmented Society'; Gans, *Gojse nijd & joods narcisme*; Gans, *Memorboek*; Gans, *Het Nederlandse Jodendom*; Kaplan, *The Dutch Intersection*; Leydesdorff, *Wij hebben als mens geleefd*; Leydesdorff, 'The Veil of History'; Meijer, *Hoge hoeden, lage standaarden*; Michman, Beem, Michman, *Pinkas*; Schöffer, 'Nederland en de joden in de jaren dertig in historisch perspectief'; Sijes,

a segment of Dutch society, without losing all its characteristics, while Jews also influenced general life. For example, through their use of language; they abandoned Yiddish as their vernacular and adopted Dutch, sometimes spoken with a typical pronunciation and peculiar composition. However, many Yiddish words survived and made it into the everyday Dutch used by non-Jews, including besides *Mokum* terms such as *ponem* (face), *tof* (decent), *sof* (flop) and *gein* (fun).

However, integration was hampered and partially reversed during the 1930s. This segregation had three causes. First, the global depression that followed the 1929 Wall Street crash brought widespread unemployment and renewed poverty to the Netherlands. A by-product of the economic crisis was the resurfacing jealousy in the general population about outsiders such as Jews who competed for the limited opportunities for work, provisions for housing and entitlements to social benefits. Occasionally, Jews were made scapegoats for the misery. Second, as stated earlier, Hitler's ascent to power in neighbouring Germany in 1933 and his subsequent persecution of Jews culminated in the arrival of thousands of Jewish refugees in the Netherlands,[4] and they were increasingly regarded as undesirable. Third, the rise of National Socialism in the Netherlands increased the expression of hatred of Jews. Most Dutch people rejected anti-Semitism, but anti-Jewish feelings seeped into contemporary thinking.

On the eve of war in 1939, Jews were once again seen as a separate group. Prejudices resurfaced and new bias emerged. It was voiced in hurtful jokes, as had been the custom in the past, and in abusive terms such as *jodenneus* (Jewish nose) or *smous* (Jew). The Netherlands didn't witness organised and large-scale anti-Jewish violence, but Jews noticed once again that they stood out. Children encountered this at an early age. The Dutch cabaret artist Louis Davids worded the experience in his song *The Jewish Child*[5] about a boy called Bram, short for Abraham:

Little Bram, a slight Jewish boy, cries out loud.
Doesn't understand
Why his mates bait and annoy him,
Fool him and mock him.
Mum, he asks, why do they call me Jew?

Studies over jodenvervolging, 128–30; Tammes, Scholten, 'Assimilation of Ethnic-Religious Minorities in the Netherlands; Wallet, *Nieuwe Nederlanders*.
4. Moore, *Refugees from Nazi Germany in the Netherlands, 1933–1940*.
5. The song can be found on the compilation album *Louis Davids, de grote kleine man*, EMI-disc 128–25 571–72 (translation by author). See also Peekel, Groot, *Louis Davids*.

She lifts the boy onto her lap and tells him not to cry, but to learn and bear himself: 'Just play on your own, *gebensjte* (blessed) boy,' she soothes. 'And be proud to be mummy's Jewish child.' In the final verse she sings:

> Listen dear little Bram:
> The fate of Jewish children isn't all sunny,
> But later, when you're big,
> You'll understand that you're Jewish.
> And that good people don't hurt us Jews.
> C'mon, dry your tears, Bram.

As their participation in the general economy and social life of the Netherlands retreated during the 1930s, many Jewish workers remained caught in traditional occupations in the diamond, tobacco, bakery, confectionary, textile and tailoring industries. That is, if they were able to hang on to their predominantly low-paid jobs. Unemployment brought paucity. Other Jews continued or returned to work as market traders and street vendors, who also suffered severely from poverty. Some persisted as merchants and shopkeepers, who were usually struggling. A few held on to positions as financiers, owners and managers in the traditional industries, which sometimes flourished. In addition, proportionally many Jews worked as doctors, lawyers, teachers and journalists, because the economic sectors in which these people operated traditionally had few entry barriers for Jews.

In politics, Jews were members of the Liberal, Social Democratic, Communist and Revolutionary Socialist parties. Few joined the various Christian Democratic parties, which until 1939 almost single-handedly governed the Netherlands and welcomed only baptised Jews. The Social Democrats exercised influence in local politics, notably in the main cities, but held no Dutch government posts until 1939. Nevertheless, through their union work and municipal administration, the Socialists influenced and attracted large numbers of Jews. Although Communism was discredited and later lost all credibility – as Ter put it: 'In our home Stalin's portrait hung upside down'[6] – the Communist party in the Netherlands at the time still had comparatively many Jewish members and was appealing to young Jews. This resulted from the Communist outspokenness and preparedness to take action, for example, in the popular unrest against the reduction of unemployment benefit in 1934, when barricades were erected in Amsterdam and five protesters were killed by the military and police, or in the street fighting with Dutch National Socialists that occurred occasionally during the second half of the 1930s.

---

6. Interview T. Kolthoff.

The Dutch Zionists, despite their organisational talent, widespread support among Jews and international influence, held little political sway at government level. Among them new disputes arose. The younger generation was seeking what they regarded as a purer form of Zionism, less diluted with non-Jewish values and habits and more radically aimed at emigration to Palestine. Several young Dutch Jews and refugees from Germany joined the Palestine Pioneers, who were actively preparing for *aliyah* (emigration to Palestine). The generational gap as well as the increasingly precarious position in which many Jews found themselves contributed to the intensity of the conflicts among the Dutch Zionists.

However, integration did advance in some areas. After the resurfacing prejudices, during the years just before the Second World War several groups in the Dutch society started thinking in more positive terms about Jews. As a result of the oppression of the Jews in Germany and the flood of refugees, some Protestant and Roman Catholic individuals and groups rejected traditional religious bigotry and began organising practical aid for Jewish victims of persecution. In a few industry sectors more Jews found employment, for example, in margarine making, financial services and department store retail. Relatively many young Jews made their way into higher education. Although Jews were not selected for ministerial posts, some individual Jewish politicians contributed to the formulation of national policies and their implementation at local level. The art world was as always open to Jews. Finally, despite prejudice, in daily life Jews maintained contact with non-Jews. Intermarriage increased, marked by a growing number of weddings with a Jewish and a non-Jewish partner.

Within Dutch Jewry change occurred too. The 1930 census figures showed that secularisation was on the rise. Most Jews who retained religion remained Orthodox rather than joining the Reform movement. However, many ceased to visit the synagogue, even on High Holy Days. They no longer felt a need for observance or renounced religion altogether. These Jews gave shape to their identity in a manner that was determined by individual needs and preferences, for example, through maintaining ties with other Jews, continuing to refuse traditionally forbidden food like pork and using colourful language that some thought vulgar because it was deemed grammatically incorrect, while others found it flowery because it sang.

The Jewish population of the Netherlands was thereby characterised by great diversity. There were stark differences between, for example, town and country, young and old, men and women, rich and poor, illiterate and educated, religious and atheist, and conservative, liberal and left-wing. The multiplicity was one of the reasons why Jews in the Netherlands reacted differently to the persecution they encountered during the German occupation of the country. The manner in which Nol and Ter escaped the clutches of their enemies illustrates how that played out.

Chapter 2

THE WEDDING

The date of the wedding was 12 June 1940. Just over a month earlier German armies had invaded the Netherlands, which had remained neutral since war broke out in Europe in 1939. Despite the German occupation, Ter and Nol proceeded with their planned marriage. If you'd known Nol, you'd have expected an exuberant party, but we know nothing about the event. The couple look happy together on photos, but the atmosphere at the wedding was probably rather lethargic, because there was sadness, fear and insecurity in the couple's family and among their friends. This chapter introduces you to the main characters in this story and explains their trepidation.

Tertia Kolthoff was a quiet, pensive and sensitive woman, but she could be outspoken when she'd made up her mind. Talking about her family, she often mentioned 'outside loos',[1] meaning that her people originated in the country-side where homes didn't yet have indoor toilet facilities. Her father, Eliazer, had been born in 1872 in Hoogeveen, a small town in the eastern province of Drenthe. He was the son of a local trader. Her mother, Cis, was half a year younger. She was the daughter of a grain merchant and cattle dealer from Vierlingsbeek, a village in the southern province of North Brabant. Eliazer and Cis had been married there in 1900, settled in Amsterdam and had three children.

Tertia was born on 5 January 1913, a late arrival, more than 10 years younger than her brothers Mark and Frits. The official Tertia became the everyday Ter. After the retirement of her father as chief accountant of a large general department store in 1937, Ter's parents moved from their flat in the Rubens Street in Amsterdam-South to a house in the Lemon Street of the

---

1. Interview T. Kolthoff. The data on births, deaths and residence of her forebears as well as other individuals mentioned in this book come from Biografisch Woordenboek van Nederland (http://resources.huygens.knaw.nl/bwn1880-2000), Biografisch Woordenboek van het Socialisme en de Arbeidersbeweging in Nederland (https://iisg.amsterdam/en), Joods Biografisch Woordenboek – Joden in Nederland in de twintigste eeuw (www.jodeninnederland.nl) and Digitaal Monument Joodse Gemeenschap in Nederland (https://www.joodsmonument.nl).

well-to-do Fruit District of The Hague. They may have moved to The Hague because a brother of Cis, Fred van Oss – a retired magazine editor and publisher – lived there. By the time of the move, Ter had already left home and was training to become a nurse.

In December 1939 Ter had met her husband-to-be, Arnold Bueno de Mesquita, five years older, born on 23 February 1908. Nol, short for Arnold, complemented Ter handsomely. He was outgoing, warm-hearted and fun-loving, with an artistically creative mind and a touch of eccentricity. His parents, Mozes and Esther, were both born in Amsterdam, in 1868 and 1880. One of Nol's grandmothers had come from Lochem in the province of Gelderland. The other grandparents were from Amsterdam. Esther's father worked for the bankers Texeira de Mattos. Mozes and Esther had been married in 1906, when Mozes worked as decorator, but he eventually established a furnishings business. Nol had a younger brother and a sister, Izaak and Mathilde.

Initially Nol followed in his father's footsteps, but then he deviated slightly by setting up The Agency for Interior Architecture. He was possibly also an agent for Metz & Company, a department store that introduced avant-garde interior design to its wealthy Amsterdam clientele. Nol's agency was based at the address of his parents, 123 Nieuwe Herengracht,[2] where he and Ter moved into an upstairs apartment after the wedding.

Nol's parents were both descendants of Sephardi Jews who centuries earlier had left Portugal and Spain to settle in Amsterdam. The Portuguese Synagogue was just round the corner of the Nieuwe Herengracht. This was where Nol had received a Jewish upbringing. His father was devoutly religious. Ter's ancestors were Ashkenazi Jews who had lived in areas such the Rhineland before their migration to Central and Eastern Europe, from where later many travelled to Western Europe. One of her grandmothers came from Germany, the families of the other grandparents had lived for many generations in the Netherlands. Ter had also been brought up in a typically Dutch-Jewish manner. In addition to a general primary school, she went to a Jewish school, where on Wednesday afternoons and Sunday mornings the children were taught rudimentary elements of Judaism, such as the main religious habits and rules, an outline of Jewish history and some Hebrew.

What did it mean for them to be Jewish? Nol saw it as follows:

> I feel Jewish. I'm married to a Jewish woman. Not Orthodox, not in the church, not Zionist. If not that, what is Jewishness? Jews are human, they have negative and positive characteristics. Judaism isn't a religion, not a race. It's a rhythm. It's *gein* [fun] and warmth. Some Jews have

---

2. Advert *Nieuw Israëlietisch Weekblad* 14 June 1940.

Illustration 4. Nol advertised his interior design business in the *Nieuw Israëlietisch Weekblad* on 14 June 1940.

written off Judaism on the basis of their principles. However, they're more Jewish than they imagine. Intellectually they've suppressed it, but emotionally they're Jews.[3]

Family ties were important in this Jewish identity. If a party atmosphere was lacking from the wedding of Nol and Ter, it was partly due to family circumstances. Nol's father had died in 1935. In the year preceding the marriage, the father of Ter had passed away. Both men died at a relatively young age, which increased the sadness about losing them.

Furthermore, Ter and Nol were fearful. They had been astonished by the persecution of Jews in Germany before the war. After Hitler's rise to power in 1933, Jews were forcefully removed from German public life and lost their civil rights, their property was stolen, they were assaulted, thousands were incarcerated in concentration camps and hundreds were murdered. Initially, most non-Jews in the Netherlands showed concern about the developments in the neighbouring country, but the attention for the persecution subsided, to awake again when new maltreatment took place. However, it frightened Dutch Jews all the time, despite seeming far removed from their daily life. The Zionist and historian Abel Herzberg witnessed the fear and noted:

---

3. Interview A. Bueno de Mesquita.

As it increasingly worried the Jews in the Netherlands, it was increasingly exorcised with formulas like 'It will not come, it will not come' or 'This cannot happen here in Western Europe and certainly not in the Netherlands'. And who ever predicted that it would come, and could happen, was accused of inducing fear, while they were only expressing the fear that had hung in the air over the Jews in the Netherlands since 1929 and really since 1933 and that was justified. But they did what all people do: they knew very well what was threatening them and closed their eyes.[4]

Ignoring the approaching doom became impossible after the Germans invaded the Netherlands. In a lightning strike, German army units crossed the Dutch border in the very early morning of 10 May 1940. At four o'clock Nol and Ter heard German airplanes above Amsterdam, accompanied by explosions and cannon fire. People in Amsterdam-South were woken up by the deafening noise of a German fighter plane flying over, firing from all its guns. Amsterdam's Schiphol Airport was set alight. Two days later a bomb hit one of the city's canal streets, resulting in dozens of victims.

By and large the Netherlands were ill prepared for the ordeal, despite the general mobilisation of the Dutch army in 1939. The military surrendered after four days of fighting and a German threat to destroy the main cities, following an extensive bombardment of the centre of Rotterdam. The Dutch government fled to London, leaving a population in disbelief, dejection and despair. There was widespread uncertainty and dread about what was to come. Jews shared these feelings but also expected that the National Socialists would repeat in the Netherlands the pogroms they had unleashed in Germany. Thousands of Dutch citizens escaped to England or the as yet unoccupied parts of Belgium and France, but the vast majority of the Jews could or would not escape.[5] On 15 May, Ter and Nol saw German troops entering Amsterdam.

The Germans imposed their regime in the Netherlands with competing elements from their armed forces, intelligence, security and police services. Dutch National Socialists also strove for power. The Dutch civil service, headed by departmental secretaries general, was mostly left intact and implemented German decrees. The population at large remained unclear about the intentions of the occupiers. Initially, in an effort to gain the trust of the Dutch, the Germans allowed daily life to resume its seemingly normal

---

4. Herzberg, *Kroniek de Jodenvervolging*, 15–6.
5. De Jong, *Het Koninkrijk der Nederlanden in de Tweede Wereldoorlog*, vol. VII, 358; Michman, Beem, Michman, *Pinkas*, 204.

course. In most people's eyes the occupiers now appeared to act correctly. After the violation of Dutch neutrality, the four days of warfare and the bombardment of Rotterdam, this apparent correctness brought for some a sense of relief.

However, for Jews the future remained bleak. They could only wait in fear. The expected pogroms failed to materialise, but occasionally German soldiers and Dutch National Socialists attacked people who in their eyes had a Jewish appearance. And the authorities announced measures that concerned Jews. Furthermore, the German police arrested well-known Jews, including politicians and labour leaders.

One of these arrests concerned Sara Cato 'Selma' Meyer.[6] Selma had been born in Amsterdam in 1890. She was director of the Holland Typing Office. Politically, Selma had been active as a Social Democrat and secretary of the Women's International League for Peace and Freedom. In 1936, she became chairperson of the Wuppertal Committee, an organisation set up to defend opponents of National Socialism who were arrested and tried in Germany. Her company produced the Committee's newsletter, which was distributed in four languages across Europe. Later it helped to publish the magazine *Kameradschaft* for young Germans in political exile. Selma was also involved in helping German refugees and children fleeing the Spanish Civil War (1936–39). Early in 1940, her company assisted in the distribution of clandestine leaflets in Germany. On 26 October 1940, the German police arrested Selma. She was questioned in The Hague and sent to Berlin. There she was assaulted, contracted peritonitis and following an operation Selma died in February 1941.

Such arrests affected Nol and Ter. Ter had strong political convictions, just like her brother Mark – Frits had emigrated to Canada in 1926. Mark was a fine art painter. In 1931 he had been the instigator of the Association of Workers Photographers, a group of left-wing artists. Ter was a member of the Communist Party of the Netherlands. After the German invasion in May 1940 the Communists found it difficult to determine their position. They had long regarded the National Socialists as very threatening enemies. However, confusion reigned since the signing of the Molotov-Ribbentrop Pact in August 1939, when the Soviet Union and Germany concluded a non-aggression agreement. Following the Soviet leadership, after the signing of the Pact, the Dutch Communist party endorsed neutrality instead of hostility in relation to Nazi-Germany.[7] This stance caused an end to the collaboration between Communists and other opponents of National Socialism, which already

---

6. De Cort, *Van vrouwen, vrede en verzet*.
7. Pelt. *Vrede door revolutie*, 10.

had been difficult but now became impossible. After 10 May 1940, the neutral stance maintained by the party seemed odder still, even to its members. Nevertheless, to the surprise of many, the German occupiers initially failed to act against the party; it was not outlawed until 20 July 1940. On 15 May, the Communist leaders decided to make use of the opportunities for legal activities. However, at the same time they took secret measures to prepare for illegal actions, for example, by building an apparatus of small groups or cells of people who were not widely known as party members.[8]

The political uncertainty was hard to bear. At first Ter was confused by the position on legality taken by the Communist leaders, but this changed when she was engaged in the preparation of illegal work. The party had pre-war experience with clandestine activity, for example, with secret units of civil servants for whom party membership was prohibited. The Communists had also aided refugees from Germany who stayed in the Netherlands without residence permits or who were politically active in secret – it was forbidden for refugees to be actively involved in politics. Furthermore, during the Spanish Civil War, the Communists had recruited volunteers who fought in the International Brigade on the Republican side, after which they formed groups of these volunteers who returned to the Netherlands and lost their Dutch nationality because participation in the Spanish Civil War was outlawed for Dutch citizens. In May 1940, party organisers called upon members who had been involved in these activities. Ter was one of them.

In addition, Nol and Ter were already engaged in another illicit pursuit, which put them in serious danger after the German invasion – hiding people who were wanted by the German police. They had become involved in this activity through a friend of Nol. Nol had lots of friends. He was, in his own words: 'Somebody who found it easy to make new friends. Many people came to my parents' home for parties. Also non-Jews.'[9]

The friendship, which pulled Nol and Ter into an activity that was already illegal before May 1940 and became dangerous after the German invasion, had arisen from Nol's interest in cabaret. Several years before the war, Nol went to see a cabaret performance in an Amsterdam theatre. The artists and their audience consisted of Jews and non-Jews, and among the Jews were refugees from Germany. There was a ball afterwards: 'They danced, but the Dutch people felt inhibited and didn't dance with the Germans.'[10] This reflected the negative feelings that existed about German Jews. You heard,

---

8. Galesloot, Legêne, *Partij in het verzet*, 43–99, 68, 92, 129–30, 134; De Keizer, 'De CPN illegaal'; Hensen, 'Het verzet van links', 91–4.
9. Interview A. Bueno de Mesquita.
10. Interview A. Bueno de Mesquita.

for example, that the German Jews 'had caused the persecution themselves because of their haughty attitude' or about German Jewish refugees 'always boasting how much better everything had been at home'.[11] Some of this prejudice was shared by Dutch Jews, but not by Nol who did dance with German-Jewish girls.

One of the girls was cabaret artist Irmgard 'Irmschen' Levi. During the summer of 1934 she performed under the *nom de plume* Irmgard Andersen in the Kurhaus, a venue in the coastal resort of Scheveningen near The Hague. One of her songs was *The Trapeze Artist*. Nol saw the show, loved Irmschen's performance and found her extremely attractive. He fell in love when they met. The girl came from a wealthy German Jewish environment, but in the Netherlands Irmschen had to look for a menial job after the openings in the world of cabaret were exhausted. She started selling cigarettes and chocolate in cinemas and at party evenings, and performed only in private.

Nol's first date with Irmschen was to a cabaret where the well-known German singer Dora Gerson performed. Dora sang *Momente So, Momente So*. It was a German song about the trials and tribulations of the refugee existence: '*Heute hast du noch fünf Zimmer / Morgen bist du Kohlentrimmer*' (Today you have five rooms / Tomorrow you're trimming coals).[12] Nol admired Dora's interpretation of the song and asked Irmschen if she could match it: 'She answered: "Dora does it so and so" – large arm gestures – "and she does it so. It isn't easy." But Irmschen could do it well.'[13] Nol also went with Irmschen and her sister to the beach at Scheveningen. He made up an excuse to stay away from work in his father's shop and had a marvellous time: 'Two beautiful girls beside me. Wonderful, wonderful. In the sand-dunes I listened to their entire repertoire. I was as it were their guinea pig.'[14]

However, Irmschen got an accompanist. That was pianist Nathan Notowicz, nicknamed Notto, and he stole Irmschen from Nol – later she left by boat to the United States. Nevertheless, Notto became Nol's 'best friend'.[15]

Notto came from Germany, where he had been born in 1911. He didn't speak much and was perhaps a bit shy. Although, the pianist could suddenly come up with a good joke. After delivering the punchline he squinted at you. That, Nol and Ter thought, made him look very Jewish: 'With Notto you

---

11. IISG, *Stimmen des Hauses. Von den Gäste, für die Gäste* 6 December 1937; Bregstein, Bloemgarten, *Herinnering aan Joods Amsterdam*, 261, 267–8; Herzberg, *Brieven aan mijn kleinzoon*, 144–5.
12. Klöters, 'Dora Gerson en het eerste emigrantencabaret Ping Pong', 218.
13. Interview A. Bueno de Mesquita.
14. Interview A. Bueno de Mesquita.
15. Interview A. Bueno de Mesquita.

could make *minje* [from *minyan* – the quorum of ten Jewish adults needed for certain religious obligations]. He looked like ten Jews.'[16] Notto had arrived in Amsterdam shortly after Hitler's rise to power. His parents and one brother had come too. Another brother was a Zionist who emigrated to Palestine. Notto was no Zionist, which didn't mean that he denied his Jewishness. On the contrary, he was an expert on Yiddish songs and worked with Jewish cabaret artists. That's how he met Irmschen and got friendly with Nol.

Because of Notto, Nol went to the Oosteinde Home.[17] This institution had been opened in 1937 in Amsterdam as a centre for Jewish refugees. The Home's address was 16 Oosteinde, in 1939 it was expanded with the building on number 24. Both premises consisted of large nineteenth-century mansions on the even side of the street near the Frederik Square, where the Palace of People's Industry had burned. The Home welcomed refugees for entertainment and education, which was supplied through courses, meetings, lectures and cultural events. Notto was an employee of the Home and used his contacts to attract top artists for important occasions.

Nol came to the Oosteinde Home for the cabaret evenings that Notto helped to organise, but according to Nol, Notto organised a lot more: 'This boy was sent here to organise the underground work.'[18] Nol meant the work of the German Communist party. Actually, together with two other refugees, Notto was responsible for part of this work in the Netherlands, in particular to maintain contact with party members who had fled Germany, build ties with people with whom these refugees could collaborate, and care for comrades who stayed in the Netherlands without a permit. As political pursuits were illegal for all refugees in the Netherlands, Jews from Germany who wanted to be involved in politics had to hide their activity or keep their presence in the country secret. The second option meant they had secretly crossed the border, didn't register as aliens with the Dutch police or a local municipality, had no residence permission and lived therefore illegally in the Netherlands.

One of them was Joseph 'Jupp' Mahler,[19] a refugee who had selected the first option and kept his activity hidden. Jupp came from Krefeld, where he had been born in 1894 and attended a Jewish primary and a general secondary school. During the First World War, Jupp volunteered and fought in the German army. He was badly wounded and awarded the Iron Cross Second Class. Jupp was an inconspicuous and quiet man, who as printer's

---

16. Interview T. Kolthoff.
17. For more information about the Oosteinde Home see Braber, Passage naar vrijheid (1985); Braber, *Passage naar vrijheid* (1987).
18. Interview A. Bueno de Mesquita.
19. HstA RW58-869, 3933, 53199.

journeyman joined the Social Democrats. In 1922 he married Hedwig Abraham, three years younger and from Duisburg. They dreamed of starting their own print shop.

In 1935 the Mahlers fled Germany. They settled just across the Dutch border in Venlo, a town in the southern province of Limburg, where Jupp started a company named Refaka. It produced printed materials and office stationery, mostly for export to Germany. During busy periods Refaka employed some 20 people.

The Dutch police in Venlo quickly suspected Jupp of political activity. This was caused by local gossip and, more seriously, information from the German police, who told their Dutch colleagues about his former Socialist preferences and actions. Furthermore, the German police drew the attention of the Dutch to clandestine political pamphlets that appeared in Germany and were allegedly produced by Refaka.

For a month, Dutch detectives staked out the printers. They were especially interested in the people who visited the Mahlers. Among them was somebody who was said to be a Communist courier – a man called Paul. He was also suspected of making propaganda against National Socialism. Paul had been arrested earlier, but he had escaped. In the *General Police Bulletin* of 20 May 1937, the chief of police in Venlo requested his arrest. Another visitor, arrested and questioned by the Dutch police, recalled a discussion in Jupp's place: 'Furthermore, Paul told me during this debate that he had been in Russia for five years to be trained as a Communist.'[20] Unfortunately, this information found its way into the file that the German police kept on Jupp.

Indeed, the Mahlers did regularly receive visitors, including people that Notto's trio in the Oosteinde Home sent to Jupp. He helped them as much as possible, which didn't necessarily mean that he was engaged in Communist activity. Later he told a reporter of the Dutch Social Democratic newspaper *The People*: 'It doesn't interest me at all which political vision these people support. They may support Catholicism, Communism, Socialism or Judaism. The only thing that matters to me is that they're persecuted by National Socialism.'[21]

The paper printed the interview on 7 July 1937. The reason for publication was an action of the Dutch police. They had raided Jupp's premises and during the search officers found pamphlets and Marxist literature. As a result he was declared 'unwanted foreigner'. Jupp and Hedwig had to leave the Netherlands. *The People* protested against the extradition. The paper found the accusation of spreading Communist propaganda unproven and argued that

---

20. HstA RW58-869.
21. *Het Volk* 7 July 1937. See also *Nieuwe Venlosche Courant* 30 June 1937.

bureaucratic arbitrariness had prevailed. It noted that the deportation had been hurried, leaving the Mahlers no time to liquidate their business properly. *The People* suggested the police had overstepped their authority and urged the government to 'seriously investigate the performance of the Venlo Chief of Police'.[22]

Meanwhile, the Mahlers moved to Belgium, but their life there ran far from smoothly. Hedwig may have been involved in smuggling. In March 1940, the Belgian authorities returned the couple to the Netherlands, where the police immediately transferred them across the German border into the hands of the German police, who had maintained a lively interest, assisted by their colleagues in Venlo. A German report said: 'The Dutch investigators have done their utmost to learn from Mahler with which Communist cells he was dealing at home and abroad. Mahler is a very active Communist agent.'[23] The outlook for Jupp and Hedwig was obviously very bleak, but we'll meet them again later.

The misfortune of the Mahlers shows how dangerous it was for German refugees in the Netherlands to be involved in political activity, even before the outbreak of war. By 1940, a few hundred refugees concealed their stay in the Netherlands, mostly Social Democrats and Communists, and a relatively large number of them were Jewish. They had to be cared for.

Notto's trio in the Oosteinde Home organised small groups of young people to provide some of this care. For example, the refugees lived with Dutch families, including many households where the breadwinner was unemployed and who were poor themselves. So the supply of food was important, but it was to be provided covertly. The people in the Oosteinde Home collected provisions and money. Notto's youngsters distributed the food. They usually knew the Dutch families, but they didn't know the refugees by name and hardly ever saw them. The youngsters also took supplies to addresses where refugees only came to eat. Sometimes refugees had a permanent place to sleep, where they received a pot of soup or a panful of prepared food that could be heated on a small stove. Or they ate on rotating days with different families.[24]

In 1939, once he got to know him well enough, Notto asked Nol if he could find people to help care for the illegal refugees. Nol was eager to assist, but Ter was more careful. She first asked her party comrades whether this was allowed. The answer was that Notto could be trusted, he had a good reputation amongst the Dutch Communists. After getting party permission, Ter involved one of her friends in this work. That was Trudel Van Reemst-De Vries.

---

22. *Het Volk* 7 July 1937.
23. HstA RW58-869.
24. Interviews M. Rubinstein and U. Rubinstein-Littmann, and A. Stertzenbach-David.

We don't know how and when Ter and Trudel first met, but as they were both nurses and politically active, it's obvious that their first meeting occurred in the pre-1940 health care or at a political event. What we do know[25] is that Trudel had a strong-willed personality and liked to make up her own mind, even if this caused problems and turned her into an outcast. She was a bit of an outsider anyway. Trudel had been born in 1914 in Frankfurt am Main in Germany. Her father was Dutch and her mother came from France. In 1925 the family moved to the Netherlands. She was raised in a traditional Jewish manner and joined an Orthodox Zionist youth movement, until she broke with the Zionists in 1933, apparently after a conflict about the position of the Arabs in Palestine. Trudel was a qualified pharmacist's assistant, but because of a lack of vacancies, she accepted a position as student nurse in a hospital in Rotterdam.

After the start of the Spanish Civil War Trudel wanted to go to Spain, but her father objected:

That Sunday afternoon I phoned my parents, asking if they wanted to come by in the evening. I received them in my room. It was awkward. Suddenly my father said: 'Should you not be going to the hospital? You're in the night shift, aren't you?' I told them that I wasn't going back to the hospital, that I'd run away and would depart for Spain the day after tomorrow. It was the only time in my life that my father banged the table with his fist: 'That is not going to happen.' My mother said: 'If she says she's going, she'll go.'[26]

Trudel did travel to Spain, where she worked as a hospital nurse. It was hard work, especially with transports arriving from the front. Trudel nursed on a ward for patients with throat, nose, eye and ear wounds. Among the casualties were people whose jawbones had been blown off, which made a deep impression on her – after all, Trudel was just a student nurse, never mind being trained for work in a frontline hospital. They were short of everything. She put the wounded to bed and gave them pyjamas, but there was no change of underclothes or bedlinen and only 'two thermometers for the entire ward'.[27]

In Spain, Trudel got to know Theo 'Red' van Reemst. As his nickname suggests, Theo was a Communist. He was a doctor, fought on the Republican side, had been wounded and came as a recovering patient to Trudel's hospital

---

25. Interview T. van Reemst-De Vries.
26. Interview T. van Reemst-De Vries.
27. Interview T. van Reemst-De Vries.

in Villa Nueva de la Jarra. They fell in love and were married by the local mayor. Officially, Trudel and Theo didn't get married until later, on 25 January 1939, after they returned to the Netherlands from Spain. Following the Dutch ceremony Theo took over half a general practitioner's practice in a working-class neighbourhood in Amsterdam. Trudel heard that she wasn't allowed to finish her nursing training, apparently because now she was a married woman.

At Ter's instigation, Trudel got in touch with Notto. The connection was maintained when, in the summer of 1939, Trudel and Theo moved to a new medical practice in Vlaardingen, a small town on the Meuse, west of Rotterdam. Trudel collected food, mostly durable articles in tins, destined for refugees in hiding. She received the goods from prominent residents of Vlaardingen, a circle to which she had access because of Theo's status in the health service. Once a month somebody came from Amsterdam to collect a suitcase full of provisions. Trudel also found shelter for refugees and she and Theo took people into their home, including five persons who were illegally staying in the Netherlands and didn't possess identity papers or resident permits.

Among other young Jews who were involved in this care work was Judith 'Juud' Oostenbroek.[28] She was a lively person, occasionally a bit nervous, somebody with what you'd call 'a heart of gold'. She had been born in 1920 in The Hague, but lived in Amsterdam, where she studied to become a social worker. Together with her sister Iens, Juud collected money for Polish refugees.

Juud got to know Ter and Nol through Hans Wolf, a conscript in the Dutch army. Hans had been born in 1909 in Amsterdam. He came from a wealthy Jewish family; his father ran a flourishing furnishings business. Hans worked as a photographer and was well known among artists. At the end of 1929 he and his brother-in-law Mark Kolthoff, Ter's sibling, founded a Dutch branch of *Les Amis du Monde*, a cultural association that attracted political activists. In 1931 Hans joined the Association of Workers Photographers. He lived in a commune in a suburb of The Hague. When in August 1939 the Dutch government announced the general mobilisation of the armed forces, Hans was called up and sent to the North Sea harbour of IJmuiden, where he served as a private in the Signals Corps. During this posting he met Juud. Hans put her in touch with Nol and Ter and they introduced Juud to the care organisers in the Oosteinde Home.

Juud made new friends in the Home. A few of them were members of Anski, a cultural organisation of Polish Jews. Some of the Poles were Communists and mixed freely with German refugees. One of the young Jewish Communist Poles was Sera Anstadt. She had been born in Lwów in 1923. Later she wrote

---

28. Interview J. Wolf-Oostenbroek.

about this time, when they enjoyed sport and walking, but she also remembered spending much time on politics: 'The political training was conducted by refugees who had gained experience in the movement in Germany.'[29] She also noted: 'Secrecy, discipline and tenacity were the main strengths of the [Communist] party' and 'we learned quickly that orders had to be obeyed.'[30] As we shall see later, she was going to regret being obedient.

Two young German-Jewish refugees who went to Anski events were Uschi Littmann and her boyfriend Max Rubinstein. Both had been born in 1920, respectively in Berlin and Düsseldorf. The experience of persecution in Germany and their flight to the Netherlands, where the couple met, had given Uschi and Max a desire to speak up and act against injustice.[31] They had a lot in common – in their friendly, open-minded and warm-hearted manner Uschi and Max eagerly absorbed the new impressions, grasped the novel opportunities that presented themselves in Amsterdam and found like-minded people in Anski.

Among them were Bella and Floor Przyrowski, who had been born in 1922 and 1927, respectively. The sisters had Polish-Jewish parents. Bella was outgoing and lively, and she brought friends to their home. In contrast, Floor was a quiet and withdrawn child, but she enjoyed going with Bella to Anski and the Oosteinde Home.[32] Later she visited the Home on her own and got used to engaging with people. That's how she got to know boys from the Jewish Work Village New Gate[33] in the Wieringermeer polder, situated in the far north-east of the province of North Holland. These were mostly German Jews, including Palestine Pioneers who were training to become agricultural workers in preparation for *aliyah*. The training took place in the polder, but during some weekends they were given time off and permission to travel to Amsterdam.

Like Uschi and Max, Floor and Bella took part in the care work. The Polish girls were engaged through Bella's boyfriend, Ernst Levy. In the eyes of the young Jews, Ernst wasn't only a bit older and possibly wiser but also 'obsessed with politics'.[34] He had been a deputy manager and travelling salesman for his father's fur business in Hamburg, where he had been born in 1914. Ernst became a member of Notto's trio, responsible for the care work.

---

29. Anstadt, *Een eigen plek*, 61. See also her brother's autobiography: Anstadt, *Kruis of munt*.
30. Anstadt, *Een eigen plek*, 61.
31. Interview M. Rubinstein and U. Rubinstein-Littmann.
32. Interviews F. Brandon-Przyrowski and T. Kolthoff.
33. Interviews F. Brandon-Przyrowski and G. Laske; Buijs; 'The Werkdorp Corresspondence'; Moore, *Refugees from Nazi Germany in the Netherlands, 1933–1940*, 48–51, 94; Stegeman, Vorsteveld, *Het joodse werkdorp in de Wieringermeer 1934–1941*.
34. Interview F. Brandon-Przyrowski.

The third member of the leadership was Alice Heymann-David. She had been born in 1909 in Dortmund, had studied Dentistry and was married. Following Hitler's rise to power she devoted herself to underground work in the German city of Cologne. Alice was forced to flee from Germany after her husband was arrested and disappeared in jail. What she witnessed in Germany attracted Alice in the Netherlands to Selma Meyer's Wuppertal Committee and made her even more determined and single-minded, 'completely focussed on the overthrow of National Socialism'.[35] To earn a living Alice worked as secretary and deputy director of the Oosteinde Home.

Notto, Ernst and Alice most likely formed a cell of the German Communist party. Their objective was of course the realisation of their political ideals, but through the prevailing circumstances most of the practical activity of the trio evolved into building an organisation to care for illegal refugees. After the German occupation of the Netherlands in May 1940 that work was continued and extended, while it adopted an even greater secrecy, some of which would pay off later.

The imminent danger for refugees caused by Germans troops arriving in Amsterdam had an impact on Ter and Nol as they were preparing to get married. Nol received a message from Notto. Could he come by to discuss an urgent matter? Notto couldn't get out. On the eve of the invasion, German nationals had been ordered to stay at home by the Dutch authorities. A few political refugees had been interned on 19 April 1940, others like Notto apparently had house arrest, which appeared to have been extended a month later. Nol went to see Notto: 'It was a fantastic moment in these troublesome May days. He wanted to know if together we could do something against these rotters.'[36] After that conversation Nol and Ter took in two German refugees at Notto's request.

The German-Jewish refugees in the Netherlands who were politically active were worried that they would be rounded up by the Dutch authorities and handed over to the German army or that the German police would come to arrest them – after all, many of the addresses of those who kept their activity but not their presence secret were registered by the Dutch police and municipal agencies.

The fear of arrest among German Jews in Amsterdam wasn't groundless. On 29 May 1940, a post of the German political police was opened in an office on the Herengracht, only a short walk from Nol and Ter's home. Several officials in this *Aussenstelle* of the *Befehlshaber der Sicherheitspolizei und des Sicherheitsdienst* (SD) had before May 1940, from bases in western Germany, spied on German

---

35. Interview A. Stertzenbach-David.
36. Interview A. Bueno de Mesquita.

refugees who stayed in the Netherlands. Among these officials was the then *SS-Untersturmführer* Klaus Barbie[37] from the *Oberabschnitt-West* of the SD. In Amsterdam, he became responsible for 'Jewish affairs'. The first task of the *Aussentelle* was the 'arrest of emigrated Communists, Socialists and Jews and their transport back to Germany.'[38] Carrying out this work with enthusiasm, Barbie would become a feared persecutor and opponent of Jewish resistance.

Some refugees were able to help themselves. People such as Uschi Littmann had experienced resistance in Germany: 'We were tried and tested.'[39] She had been involved in politics from an early age as a member of a Jewish youth movement in Germany. When it was outlawed by the National Socialists, they went underground:

> We read forbidden books, made newspapers and glued strips of paper to lampposts with slogans against Fascism. We were extremely careful. We knew what happened in the concentration camps. I had a friend. Her husband was sent to the Oranienburg camp. Within half a year he was dead.[40]

So Uschi didn't underestimate the new danger, and in May 1940 she and Max Rubinstein went into hiding, using a shelter they had prepared before the German attack on the Netherlands.

Other refugees didn't have hiding places. They included the two German refugees for whom Nathan Notowicz was trying to find shelter. In Nol and Ter's apartment on the Nieuwe Herengracht they typed and printed a small clandestine magazine. 'Notto organised everything. He radiated enormous strength.'[41]

In short, this chapter shows that the occupation of the Netherlands in May 1940 and German measures and actions caused Ter and Nol to start conducting resistance work. In a sense it was a step up from their pre-1940 activity, in which they had been drawn by Nathan Notowicz, whom Nol had befriended through his love for cabaret, ability to make friends, affinity with German-Jewish refugees and affair with Irmgard Levi. Ter and Nol had

---

37. BDC: K. Barbie; WL: Klaus Barbie; NIOD 248-0354; interview J. Reutlinger; Barnouw, Brilman, *Verslag van het Rijksinstituut voor Oorlogsdocumentatie en de Landelijk Officier belast met de opsporing van oorlogsmisdadigers en andere politieke delinkwenten uit de Tweede Wereldoorlog met betrekking tot de activiteiten in Nederland van de SS-Obersturmführer Klaus Barbie*; Linklater, Hilton, Ascherson, *The Fourth Reich*, 43–54.
38. For example HStA RW58: A. Langkemper.
39. Interview M. Rubinstein and U. Rubinstein-Littmann.
40. Interview M. Rubinstein and U. Rubinstein-Littmann.
41. Interview A. Bueno de Mesquita.

enrolled some of their Jewish friends, such as Trudel van Reemst-de Vries, Hans Wolf, Juud Oostenbroek and her sister Iens, who wanted to help Jewish refugees in the Netherlands.

Others engaged in the care for illegal immigrants were German-Jewish refugees themselves, such as Max Rubinstein and Ushi Littman, who had opposed the National Socialists before fleeing from Germany and maintained a desire to act, and young Jews with a Polish background, such as Sera Anstadt and Bella and Floor Przyrowski. They got involved in various ways, for example, Bella through her boyfriend Ernst Levy. After the German invasion, Notto asked Nol whether he was prepared to do something against the occupiers, and Nol wanted to help and take action against the National Socialists. Ter was also motivated by her political convictions, while her party earmarked and engaged Ter in the preparation of illegal work. She shared her beliefs with Alice Heymann-David, Nathan Notowicz and Ernst Levy – an enterprising trio determined to play a part in an anticipated quick overthrow of the National Socialist regime, so that they'd be able return to Germany soon, a sentiment felt by many refugees. The trio built an organisation to care for illegal refugees, and after May 1940, this organisation developed into a small resistance group in and around the Oosteinde Home that consisted almost entirely of Jews.

So in June 1940 Ter and Nol not only received their wedding guests but also two houseguests. They were still sitting on the floor, because the new furniture hadn't yet been delivered, when 'Kurt' and 'Jo' came to live with them as their first two *onderduikers* (persons in hiding).[42] Many more would follow. The following chapters show how the decision to resist had more direct consequences and caused long-term reverberations, which Nol and Ter couldn't foresee.

---

42. Interview A. Bueno de Mesquita.

Chapter 3

THE RISING TIDE

On his thirty third birthday Nol narrowly escaped death. It was Sunday 23 February 1941 when he witnessed, from the window of his apartment, a raid to capture Jews: 'The Germans blocked the bridge. They grabbed everybody.'[1] Fortunately, Nol had just returned home, when the Germans started to pick up Jewish men at random from the streets of Nol's neighbourhood. Hundreds were taken and carried off. Later Nol and Ter heard that the German action was a reprisal.

What had happened that warranted this retaliation?

Following the surrender of the Dutch army in May 1940 the expected pogroms failed to materialise, but the Germans did announce and implement anti-Jewish decrees. For example, in July 1940 Jews were removed from the air-raid defence service. More serious were their dismissals in business, broadcasting and the press. In addition, Jews were hard hit by some general measures. For instance, when ritual slaughter was outlawed. Or when German citizens in the Netherlands had to report at special alien registration offices. The common response of Jews to these measures at this stage was one of apprehension, but otherwise they were trying to carry on as usual and make the best of their lives, very much like the rest of the Dutch population.[2]

This 'wait and see' attitude is understandable. From today's perspective it may seem as if the persecution of Jews in the Netherlands was stepped up in degrees – registration, segregation, isolation, deportation and extermination. However, until January 1942 the National Socialists did not execute a coherent plan for dealing with the Jews in Western Europe. The German authorities in the Netherlands took numerous measures, but for contemporaries there appeared to be little cohesion. The apparent lack of strategy was amplified by the competition between various service departments in the occupying forces and the Dutch National Socialists. This caused confusion among Jews, if not total incomprehension. It was therefore impossible for Ter and Nol to foretell

---

1. Interview A. Bueno de Mesquita.
2. Romijn, 'The War 1940–1945'. See also Barnouw, *Geschiedenis van Nederland 1940–1945*.

the results of specific German actions and to judge in advance which reactions would have the best outcomes.

Nevertheless, the tide was rising. The first anti-Jewish measures were followed in October 1940 by the so-called Aryan declaration: public sector workers had to state in this document that they weren't Jewish. Nol and Ter learned that teachers at the Amsterdam Lyceum refused to sign, but few people outside this educational establishment were prepared to take that course of action. Compliance was common. The sequel to the declaration revealed itself in November when Jewish civil servants across the country received redundancy notices. The sackings caused protests from students and staff at some universities and schools, but these isolated actions failed to trigger general resistance against the occupiers in the Netherlands.

The Germans brutally oppressed Jewish opposition to the declaration and the dismissals. Protesting Jews were arrested and sent to concentration camps, from where their death notices sometimes arrived very quickly. Well-known examples that Nol and Ter heard about were professor Leo Polak, who refused to accept his discharge from the University of Groningen, and B. Arnold Kahn, the director of an Amsterdam department store who gathered his staff and loudly protested the German measures.

Polak, born in 1880, had studied law in Amsterdam and worked in Groningen since 1928 as lecturer in philosophy. He was an eminent freethinker and opponent of National Socialism. In a letter to the university he called his dismissal an 'order of the enemy'.[3] He was arrested in February 1941, imprisoned in Groningen and Leeuwarden and died in December 1941 in the Sachsenhausen concentration camp. One of his daughters, Jetteke, born in 1921, took part in the student protests. She was arrested too, transported to Ravensbrück and died in Auschwitz in November 1942.

Kahn had been born in Amsterdam in 1886. He also studied law in Amsterdam, where he was one of the founders of the Dutch Zionist Student Organisation. Kahn later helped to establish the *Keren Hajesod* (Palestine Development Fund) in the Netherlands. He often spoke at Zionist gatherings. Kahn took over his father's firm, the renowned store of Hirsch & Co. After the announcement of an anti-Jewish measure he implored his gathered employees to remain good Dutch citizens and reject the idea that Jews could be denied legal equality. Kahn was arrested and died in May 1941 in Buchenwald.[4]

---

3. De Jong, *Het Koninkrijk der Nederlanden in de Tweede Wereldoorlog*, vol. III, 103, vol. IV, 752, 802, vol. V, 265; Presser, *Ondergang*, vol. I, 96–7.
4. Michman, Beem, Michman, *Pinkas*, 144; Giebels, *De Zionistische Beweging in Nederland 1899–1941*, 144–5.

Rabbis also spoke out. The well-known and respected rabbi Simon de Vries had set the tone in December 1940:

> From where does the strength, the inner salvation, come now? Brothers and sisters, it can only come from Judaism. From our Jewish self-consciousness. Jacob made a promise: 'When God will be with me.' That 'when' wasn't conditional but of time. It means that when the time will have come – and that time will come – that the Divine promises have been fulfilled, this stone (that Jacob used as a pillow) will be a house of God. That time has come indeed for Jacob, that is: for Israel. This way that stone can be: the cornerstone of your inner strength, the basis of your balance, the bulwark of your resistance.[5]

De Vries had been born in 1870 in a small village in the east of the Netherlands. He served the Jewish congregation in Haarlem and was a spokesman for traditional Judaism. The rabbi was addressing Orthodox Jews. He spoke just before his retirement (De Vries died in Bergen-Belsen in 1944). Philip Frank, Chief Rabbi of North Holland, was much younger. He had been born in 1910 in Hilversum, a small town in the province of North Holland, south-east from Amsterdam, and represented a younger generation of Jewish religious leaders, appealing to a wider audience including Jews who no longer identified with Orthodoxy. He stated in a Jewish weekly that the Jewish community couldn't be destroyed:

> In the course of history it has happened several times that parts of the Jewish people suffered so much in their exile that they were submerged. But there was always enough to forge a new link with the past and thus they worked despite everything with hope and trust on the future.[6]

Later, in 1943, he was taken hostage and executed as a reprisal for a resistance attack. Shortly before his execution Frank said: 'These Germans, they cannot harm us Jews, only kill us, but Jewry will survive Fascism.'[7]

Two years earlier, in January 1941 the registration of Jewish companies started, including Nol's agency. They got a German *Verwalter* – a caretaker manager. In addition, Nol and Ter were ordered to register as Jews. They obeyed this order, just like most Jews in the Netherlands – in total 160,790 persons registered, consisting of 140,522 *Volljuden* (full-Jews), 14,549 *Halbjuden*

---

5. Gans, *Memorboek*, 615.
6. Gans, *Memorboek*, 829.
7. Michman, Beem, Michman, *Pinkas*, 407.

(half-Jews) and 5,719 *Vierteljuden* (quarter-Jews), according to the yardsticks of the National Socialists, laid down, for example, in the Nuremberg Laws of 1935. Among them were 15,174 refugees from Germany, Austria and other countries occupied by the Germans.[8] Nol and Ter were deemed *Volljuden*. Their cards in the population register were stamped with a J and they received identity cards that also carried a J.

Registration made them known to their persecutors who would be able to find them quickly through their registered address, which raises the question why Nol and Ter just as almost all the Jews in the Netherlands complied with this order.

Some Dutch Jews challenged the validity of the registration by denying a Jewish identity, but only a very small minority decided not to register, including the economics student Henk van Gelderen, who later said about the manner in which he joined the Rolls Royce resistance group: 'When you look back, it's an enormous, dangerous step. But it goes gradually, each time a new small step. And I had no choice.'[9] But decisions not to register were not widely discussed. It seemed as if everybody obeyed the registration order. Many Dutch Jews simply regarded registration as a civic duty, similar to complying with the pre-war census requirements, which they had observed as loyal citizens. The fact that Dutch civil servants, not Germans, executed the registration in 1941 seemed to offer reassurance that the register wouldn't be misused. People were also afraid of the punishment they'd receive when caught not obeying a German order, which meant arrest and imprisonment in camps like Sachsenhausen and Buchenwald. Or they simply didn't see an alternative. With hindsight you can detect the danger, but early in 1941 nobody could accurately predict the outcomes of registration or failure to register. In addition, the vast majority of the Dutch population still carried out German orders, Jews didn't act differently. And why should you not get registered? After all, the information on who was Jewish was already available from the Jewish religious congregations. Finally, the registration process took several months and only once the process was well underway did it become clear that Jews were receiving identity papers stamped with a J.

---

8. De Jong, *Het Koninkrijk der Nederlanden in de Tweede Wereldoorlog*, vol. V, 496; Gans, *Memorboek*, 831; Presser, *Ondergang*, vol. I, 64, 418. In addition to the refugees from Germany, Austria and other occupied countries, there were 7,621 Jews who had another foreign nationality or were declared stateless (about 3,000 had lost their nationality, usually after fleeing from Germany or Austria).
9. Fogteloo, Gompes, 'Henk van Gelderen', 148–9; De Jong, *Het Koninkrijk der Nederlanden in de Tweede Wereldoorlog*, vol. IV, 874–5; Presser, *Ondergang*, vol. I, 54–78.

Meanwhile, black-uniformed Dutch National Socialists made their presence felt on the streets.[10] Early in 1941, they attempted to implement German measures that prohibited Jews from entering public buildings and spaces. It brought about an attack on the old Jewish neighbourhood of the capital, a few hundred metres away from the home of Nol and Ter.

Earlier National Socialists had selected the Amsterdam markets as targets for their actions. One of their papers wrote on 5 September 1940: 'Screaming and cursing Jews who swarm the markets are a nuisance for anyone who wishes the capital well.'[11] With some German support and encouragement, the National Socialists intensified their violence in 1941. Now they randomly attacked people who in their eyes resembled the Jewish stereotype. It happened, for example, on an Amsterdam tram. A witness told the police:

> Then I also saw that two men had grabbed a Jew and seriously assaulted him. One of the men, a short fat person, hung onto the Jew's back, strangled him with his left arm and boxed him repeatedly and deliberately in the face with his right fist, as it were from below upwards. While he did that, one of the other men punched the Jew deliberately and repeatedly and in the face.[12]

It seemed as if the Dutch police was powerless.

The German occupiers also introduced signs with the words 'Jews unwanted' in public spaces. Dutch National Socialists attempted to put the notices up in restaurants and bars, which caused fights, because not everybody was prepared to be told what to put on their walls and windows. On Sunday 9 February 1941, one of these altercations erupted into a street battle on the Rembrandt Square, an entertainment centre in the Dutch capital. National Socialists marched on to the square, were beaten back, returned in greater numbers accompanied by individual German soldiers, smashed windows and forcefully entered pubs to impose the ban on Jews. The last place to fall to

---

10. The reconstruction of the events in February 1941 is based on NIOD 249-0231a and b, Arch. 077, inv.nr. 1107 and 1124, Arch. 077, inv.nr. 1186 and 1187, Arch. 020, inv. nr. 5732 (VR 347/41) 13 and Arch. 001, inv.nr. 890 (9 K.St.L. 161/41); interviews B. Bluhm, B. Bril, H. Natkiel, B. Polak, L. Sanders, A. Stertzenbach-David and L. van Weezel. See also Bregstein, Bloemgarten, *Herinneringen aan Joods Amsterdam*, 311–3; Galesloot, Legêne, *Partij in het verzet*, 67, 85; Herzberg, *Kroniek der Jodenvervolging, 1940–1945*, 117; De Jong, *Het Koninkrijk der Nederlanden in de Tweede Wereldoorlog*, vol. IV, 929, 934, vol. VIII, 337f; Presser, *Ondergang*, vol. I, 78, 94–5; Sijes, *De februari-staking 25–26 februari 1941*, 53–96.
11. *Het Nationale Dagblad* 5 September 1940.
12. Sijes, *De februari-staking 25–26 februari 1941*, 65.

the National Socialists was a bar called Alcazar. The Dutch police arrived belatedly, but they withdrew when faced by German soldiers.

Encouraged by their victory on the Rembrandt Square, the National Socialists crossed the Amstel into the Jewish neighbourhood just after six o'clock at night, kicking in doors, destroying possessions and beating up people. Some Jews fought back. One of them recalled: 'We were in a pub. With snooker queues we flew at the National Socialists. One of us had a knife. Another beat a guy from the tram.'[13] There were street clashes, but when the fight-back started in earnest, the National Socialists began leaving the area and the German military police arrived to restore order. However, the damage had been done. Ter and Nol saw broken windows and heard how Jewish families reported crimes of violence and theft at the police station around the corner on the Jonas Daniël Meyer Square.

On Monday, rumours abounded that the National Socialists had announced they would be back. The Jews in the neighbourhood were distressed, but there was also an atmosphere of determination, to hit back if the National Socialists returned. A diarist captured the mood:

> Shattered windows fell on the street and in the store fronts. That was the first assault on the Jewish neighbourhood. The next day the resilience awoke. There were men on the street, trained wrestlers and boxers, and they dared to look their man in the eye.[14]

Nol and Ter saw small groups on the street, who were debating the news. Young men from the neighbourhood and from other parts of the city also met in coffee houses and bars. In the evening, an incident took place outside the Tip Top theatre in a street that ran off the Jonas Daniël Meyer Square. The police had to break up a scuffle between a small group of National Socialists and several men, including a scrap merchant from the Waterloo Square and two of his friends, who had thrown at least one of the National Socialists into a canal.

The unrest continued the next day. The question in the Jewish neighbourhood was: what to do now? It was asked on the streets and in workplaces, shops, coffee houses and pubs. Those who had fought before or were used to street fighting did most of the talking. The idea was mooted of forming defence groups, which could fight back if the National Socialists came again. Some individuals took charge and different groups were formed. The earlier-mentioned Waterloo Square scrap merchant told other men to come to his

---

13. NIOD 249-0231: J. Groenteman 12/4/1946.
14. Paape, *Bericht van de Tweede Wereldoorlog*, 550.

yard and pick a piece of metal as a weapon. Joël Cosman,[15] a trainer from the neighbourhood sport school Olympia, assembled about 50 boxers and wrestlers in his gym. They trained and worked in shifts. The group used a small haulage truck as a transport van, enabling them to move quickly in case new attacks were reported. There were other groups, usually based in pubs, and arrangements were made to get together when trouble was expected. However, despite the will to organise, there was little organisation. Hundreds of men milled the streets, coming and going, exchanging news and gossip, for example, about a National Socialist plan to attack a synagogue.

Nol and Ter were no street fighters, but one of Ter's fellow party members was among the outspoken leaders of the defence groups. That was David 'Lard' Zilverberg. He had been born in 1916 into a large family in one of the overcrowded tenements of the long, narrow streets behind the Old Sconce in Amsterdam. When employed, Lard worked as a sign painter. He wasn't tall, but you couldn't help noticing him – a political hothead with fierce eyes and a fiery voice, and a boxer who was fleet of foot and packed a punch. He told his men: 'Bring 10 of your guys and hide yourself [over there]'[16] – Lard indicated strategic street corners, but in the height of the debate not everyone listened and confusion reigned.

In the afternoon of Tuesday 11 February 1941, a fight broke out in front of a shop owned by a National Socialist on the Old Sconce. Three people were wounded. A National Socialist went by car to report the incident at the police station on the Jonas Daniël Meyer Square. A metal bar was thrown through the windscreen of his car and he drove into bystanders; three of them got hurt, one later succumbed to his injuries. It was an indication of the tense atmosphere as well as a foreboding of what was to follow that night.

It was a misty evening. Just after half past six o'clock, a formation of about 40 Dutch National Socialists left their unit's headquarters on one of the Amsterdam canals. According to a police detective, 'with the intention to march unannounced through the Jewish quarter'.[17] They were probably singing and thereby attracting even more attention. The group crossed one of the bridges into the Jewish neighbourhood and continued until they came to the Waterloo Square.

On the square they turned left, towards the uneven-numbered side and along the tram tracks (Illustration 5). From there they could have marched towards the Jonas Daniël Meyer Square, where no less than five synagogues

---

15. Bregstein, Bloemgarten, *Herinnering aan Joods Amsterdam*, 189–90, 242–4, 311–13.
16. Interview B. Bluhm; Leydesdorff, *Wij hebben als mens geleefd*, 267–9 (see also photo opposite 273 which shows Lard's father, also a commercial painter).
17. NIOD 249-0231: P.A. Kater 27/2/1941 and anonymous report 14/4/1946

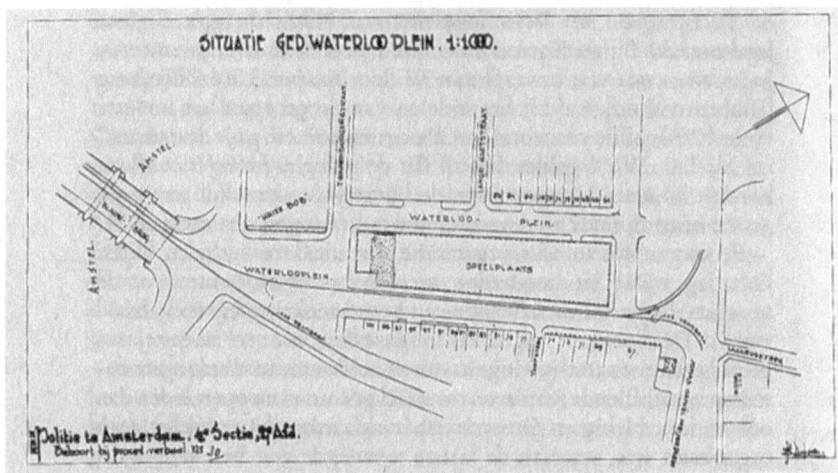

Illustration 5. A map of the Waterloo Square in a police report about the fighting on 11 February 1941. SPEELPLAATS denotes the playground around which skirmishes took place.

were shrouded in darkness. However, Jewish fighters were awaiting them, mostly hidden in doorways and side streets off the Waterloo Square. Lard and his men stood in one of the unlit alleys.

One National Socialist was on a bike. Coming onto the Waterloo Square, he took a sharp left to the even side and got separated from his group by the playground in the middle of the open space. Somebody called: 'There's one. Grab him.'[18] A piece of metal was thrown at the cyclist and it hit the man's head. Stones followed. His comrades heard the commotion and started running towards him.

At that moment the Jewish fighters emerged. Knives were drawn. Men also attacked each other with rubber hoses enforced with lead, belts, iron bars and bats, mostly hitting heads and shoulders. One of the fighters, nicknamed Jumbo, was said to have hit National Socialists in the face with pavement stones. They fought as if their lives depended on the outcome. Hatred and feelings of revenge released themselves quickly. Two men on the even side of the square saw a National Socialist named Hendrik Koot[19] on the northwest corner of the play area. One of them stated later:

---

18. Sijes, *De februari-staking 25–26 februari 1941*, 85.
19. See also P. Arnoldussen, 'Koot', *Historisch Nieuwsblad*, 8 February 2004; P. Arnoldussen, De kinderen van WA-man Hendrik Koot (http://www.paularnoldussen.nl/verhalen/koot.html).

Yes, I was there. First Koot was arguing with someone and shouted that he would wipe out the Jewish scum. We shouted back that he should try. There were several of us lined up. When one of them started the fight, they all came at the same time.[20]

They hit Koot, who fell under their blows. He stood up and tried to get away, but they grabbed him again, after which Koot succumbed.

The battle was quickly decided. Some Jewish fighters arrived almost too late: 'When we got there, some were already fighting. On the square we heard: "They're coming." All you had to do was hit the uniforms, that was a good target.'[21] Others missed the fight, which was over in minutes. The National Socialists withdrew across a bridge over the Amstel, leaving the Jewish neighbourhood.

At quarter past seven, the first wounded men arrived in a first-aid post located just off the square. The staff at this post noted their names and injuries. Koot had head wounds and the base of his skull was fractured. He was taken to hospital, where he would later die from his injuries. There were Jewish casualties too. One of them was stabbed in the upper torso. Another had a head wound and was soaked as he had fallen or was thrown into a canal. They were sent to the Jewish hospital. More injured men came to the post. At quarter past nine, the last casualty was treated. A non-Jewish man had been knocked down and beaten up. He was sent to the Jewish hospital, possibly because he had fought alongside the Jews.[22]

Meanwhile, the alarmed German police cordoned off the area. They made 20 arrests among the Jewish men who had remained on the streets, including Lard and one of his brothers. According to a witness, Lard 'still had a piece of metal in his possession'.[23] The detainees were beaten. Three of them, including Lard and his brother, were forced to pose with weapons for a propaganda photograph.[24] A few days later the Dutch police investigated Koot's death and arrested the scrap metal dealer from the Waterloo Square, but their report disappeared in a desk

---

20. NIOD 249-0231: J. Heide 18/8/1949.
21. NIOD 249-0231: J. Groenteman 12/4/1946
22. Logbook of the GG&GD (first aid) post in the Jodenbreestraat, in NIOD 249-0231.
23. NIOD 249-0231: M. Nebig 4/4/1946; interview B. Bluhm.
24. NIOD Beeldbank WO2 (http://www.beeldbankwo2) number 97205. The three were Mark van West, Lard Zilverberg and Philip Zilverberg. This is one of a series of photos, at least one of them was published. See, for example, *Het Nationale Dagblad* 18 February 1941.

draw.[25] Some of the arrested men were released. But not Lard. A year later the police started a new investigation into the disturbances. Another 20 arrests were made. Like the earlier detainees, the men were transported to Buchenwald and the Mauthausen concentration camp. Lard died there on 5 February 1942. In fact, almost all the detainees perished quickly, although the scrap metal dealer survived.

Back in February 1941, the disturbances continued, but the Dutch National Socialists transferred their actions to Amsterdam-South. In the evening of Saturday 15 February, they attacked the Koco ice cream parlour in the Rhine Street, in the neighbourhood where Ter had lived with her parents. After a short struggle the National Socialists ran off.

There were actually two Koco parlours in Amsterdam-South. One of them had been a pre-war target. A newspaper had reported that in the evening of 24 May 1939 a group of National Socialists had attacked a Jewish ice cream parlour, six of them were tried and three received prison sentences.[26] The second establishment was in the Van Wou Street. Its owners were two German Jews. In 1941 a defence group was formed to protect this parlour. They collected money and materials to make weapons such as metal pipes covered with rubber. With these arms, the defence group patrolled the streets to warn the owners when National Socialists were in the neighbourhood. It was agreed that they would try and keep any fighting away from the parlour. In case of a direct attack, the owners would turn off the inside lights and switch on a powerful outside lamp above the front door, so that the fighters could deal with the attackers. The owners would take care of the indoor defence.

Following the 1941 incident in the Rhine Street, an unknown man approached the Koco group on 18 February. He offered help and wanted to arrange a meeting with the group leaders. It was agreed he would return the next evening.

On the night of 19 February a defence group patrol returned to Koco in the Van Wou Street with a report about singing National Socialists in the neighbourhood. The owners closed the parlour. Around ten o'clock there was a knock on the door. The fighters left the parlour through the back door, followed by the owners, after they had turned off the inside lights and switched on the outside lamp.

---

25. Apparently, it has recently been retrieved in the Gemeente Amsterdam Stadsarchief (https://www.amsterdam.nl/stadsarchief/stukken/tweede-wereldoorlog/verdwenen-dossier).
26. *De Telegraaf*, 25 and 26 May, and 8 August 1939.

It's not entirely clear what happened next. In any case, the German police, not Dutch National Socialists, had banged the door. When their summons went unanswered, they must have decided to break the door down, just as the outside light went on. According to a German report,[27] as they entered the parlour, a biting gas hit their faces. It may have been that the owners had opened an ammonia gas container or that one of the Germans fired a gun when the bright outside light was switched on and blinded him, with his bullet hitting the gas flask. The commander of the German policemen declared that shots had been fired at him from within the ice cream parlour. However, the owners nor the defence group had firearms. Possibly, the German suspected or wanted to assume that the defence groups were supported by an organisation that carried guns.

Another possibility is that German officials seized the opportunity to strengthen their own position in the German hierarchy. The SS-man Klaus Barbie, for example, had contacts with Dutch National Socialists whom he encouraged to embark on daring acts, of which he could profit by instigating German repercussions when the National Socialist actions met resistance, inflating his own role. There's little doubt that Barbie played an important part. A wartime pamphlet called him *Juden-Referat*[28] (Head of the Jewish Unit) and accused him of being responsible for organising the anti-Jewish unrest.

Barbie, meanwhile promoted to *Obersturmführer*, was certainly making a successful career out of anti-Semitism. He had joined the Hitler Youth in 1933 and the SS in 1935, when he started working for the SD. Following his posting in Amsterdam in May 1940, he gathered intelligence, worked with informers and was in touch with the Dutch police. His superiors may have thought him diligent and responsible, working restlessly and intensively, but Barbie was disliked by junior officers, one of whom called him: 'An arrogant man who doesn't want to get involved with the lower ranks.'[29]

The competition between the German police, army and other service units and Dutch National Socialists for power in the Netherlands and the favour of Berlin lead to sometimes contradicting but always exaggerated German reports about the death of Hendrik Koot: 'A Jew was lying on top of Koot, biting his face with his teeth to the extent that his jaws were locked, behaving

---

27. Telex message 20 February 1941, quoted in Sijes, *De februari-staking 25–26 februari 1941*, 103.
28. Interview H. Meyer Ricard and O. V. Meyer Ricard-Haymann. The pamphlet, 'Mauthausen, 1941', was written by G. W. Dreiser (pseudonym of Grete Weil; her husband, Edgar Weil, was taken hostage in June 1941 – see below). It was published by the Hollandgruppe Freies Deutschland, which was formed by the Meyer Ricards and Grete Weil.
29. Interview K. Döring.

like a wild animal.'³⁰ Dutch National Socialists also put their oar in. A death notice in their weekly *People and Fatherland* paper said Koot 'was beastly murdered by cowardly Jewish terror'. The National Socialists further fantasised that Koot's nose and ears had been bitten off, his larynx torn by teeth and a Jew had been seen licking Koot's blood from his lips: 'The Jew has discarded his mask! Murdered? No, trampled with sadistic lust! Crushed under the ungainly feet of a nomad people that isn't of our blood.'³¹

These fantasies were of course also meant to incite the population against Jews. In reality, on 19 February, the Germans found the ice cream parlour empty. Members of the defence group were arrested next door. The two owners were caught later that night. They may have been questioned by Barbie, who would later boast that he tortured one of them. One of the owners was condemned to death and executed on 3 March 1941. This was Ernst Cahn, the first man in the Netherlands to die in front of a German firing squad.

However, that wasn't enough for the German occupiers. They formed the Jewish Council, which was ordered to appeal to the Jews of Amsterdam to surrender their arms. When Barbie's department reported that the Jews didn't answer this call, an ultimatum was set. It expired on Saturday 22 February. On that day and on Sunday 23 February, the Germans rounded up about 400 Jewish men aged between 20 and 35 from the streets of the Jewish neighbourhood – the first violent *razzia* (raid) to capture Jews in the Netherlands.³²

Nol only just escaped the raid: 'I saw these poor guys run. The Germans had blocked the bridge. There was no way out.'³³ Men were knocked from bikes, chased in streets, pursued in homes and kicked downstairs. Children were ripped from their arms. The Germans gathered their victims on the Jonas Daniël Meyer Square. They were beaten. The men had to run the gauntlet between the rifle butts of armed soldiers and the teeth of barking dogs. After that the Germans forced them to remain squatted with their hands held high. Photos were taken. It was meant to impress German superiors and frighten Jews. The general population witnessed it too, Sunday was a market day in the Jewish quarter, when many inhabitants from other neighbourhoods in Amsterdam came to browse the stalls. Eventually, the Germans took their victims away in military trucks. Only two survived, many died in the experimental gas chamber of castle Hartheim, near Mauthausen.

Klaus Barbie took part in the *razzia*, but the next day he was back in his office as normal. He received a phone call from his superiors in The

---

30. Sijes, *De februari-staking 25–26 februari 1941*, 88.
31. *Volk en Vaderland* 18 February 1941.
32. De Lang, *De razzia's van 22 en 23 februari 1941 in Amsterdam*.
33. Interview A. Bueno de Mesquita.

Hague, from where the overall German administration of the Netherlands was conducted. They wanted to know whether it was true that workers in Amsterdam would go on strike because Jews had been rounded up. There were rumours – an informer at the Fokker aviation plant had mentioned a meeting of Communists discussing the downing of tools in protest to the raid. Barbie denounced it all as bluff and exaggeration.

Despite Barbie's disbelief the Dutch population protested the next day against the *razzia* with a general strike that started in Amsterdam, spread to other cities and lasted two days. The Germans held the Jews directly responsible for the strike and summoned the Jewish Council. They threatened to execute 500 Jews if the strike didn't end. Later, more threats were issued when the Germans feared a repeat of the industrial action when they contemplated new anti-Jewish measures.

Barbie, recently awarded the *Kriegsverdienstkreuz* Second Class with Swords, remained one of the key players in the implementation of these measures. The National Socialists formed an Amsterdam branch of the *SS-Reichssicherheitshauptamt Referat IV B 4*, the department that persecuted the Jews. Barbie became its head. In addition to his scheming with Dutch National Socialists, he was about to employ even more sly methods in order to execute the policies of his Berlin masters.

On 20 March 1941, one of the chairmen of the Jewish Council was ordered to Barbie's office. This chairman was David Cohen, professor in ancient history at the Municipal University of Amsterdam. Cohen was told that a number of Jewish organisations had been dissolved and the Council had to take on their activities.[34] This measure affected Nol and Ter and their friends, because it also concerned the activity of organisations for Jewish refugees. It resulted in an action on 11 June 1941, during which one of these friends who was helping to care for illegal refugees, Max Rubinstein, managed to escape arrest, deportation and a quick death.

It started back on 20 March when the Germans cleared the Work Village New Gate in the top of North Holland, part of the measures announced to Cohen on that day. Barbie was in charge; the Work Village had to be abandoned.[35] Most of the almost 300 young German-Jewish refugees who attended agricultural training in New Gate were brought to Amsterdam by bus. After a night in a diamond factory they were taken in by Jewish families across the city. A few days later, the organisation that supported the Work Village pleaded

---

34. Cohen, 'De herinneringen van prof. dr. David Cohen', 8; Presser, *Ondergang*, vol. I, 102.
35. Stegeman, Vorsteveld, *Het joodse werkdorp in de Wieringermeer 1934–1941*, 169f; interview J. Reutlinger.

with Barbie for the return of refugees to New Gate, but initially he declined answering the plea.[36]

There was a second issue that concerned Cohen and caused him to contact Barbie. This was news about the men who had been rounded up on 22 and 23 February. They had been deported to Germany, and from there death notices of some of the men had arrived in Amsterdam. The noted causes of death appeared strange and worrying, including cardiac arrest for a young man who had been healthy and appendicitis in an even younger man whose appendix had been removed long ago.[37] The chairman of the Jewish Council asked Barbie whether anything could be done for the men who were still alive. This issue was discussed in further correspondence and meetings, which were carefully prepared by the Council, but the specific questions asked by Cohen about the deportees didn't get any decisive answers from Barbie.

However, on 9 June the impression arose of a possible resolution of the New Gate issue. On that day Barbie told Cohen and a representative of the Work Village organisation that the trainees were to be returned to the Wieringermeer. Perhaps the Jewish Council could inform the refugees, so that they wouldn't be frightened when somebody appeared at the door of the family where they stayed. Barbie also needed their addresses. Could the Council compile a list of their names and the places where they stayed? Cohen and the Work Village representative consented.[38]

They had fallen in Barbie's carefully laid trap.

Two days later, on 11 June, Max Rubinstein was taking food to illegal refugees. He and his girlfriend Uschi Littmann had long left the hiding place they had set up in May 1940 and returned to their home. On the way back from the refugees, Max suddenly saw his Uschi on a bridge across the Amstel. She rushed up to him. Two men had been at their door, asking for Max. Uschi had answered, fortunately Max wasn't in, but she suspected that they'd hang around or return, and therefore Uschi decided to come part of the way and meet Max to warn him not to go home. Just to be sure, Max stayed away from their house. Uschi's suspicion was justified when they found out that some of their friends, young German Jews, had been rounded up.

---

36. Interview A. Herzberg; Cohen, 'De herinneringen van prof. dr. David Cohen', 8–9; Stegeman, Vorsteveld, *Het joodse werkdorp in de Wieringermeer 1934–1941*, 122–3; Wasserstein, *The Ambiguity of Virtue*, 113–14.
37. Pamphlet, 'Mauthausen, 1941'.
38. Cohen, 'De herinneringen van prof. dr. David Cohen', 8; Somers, *Voorzitter van de Joodse Raad*, 104; Stegeman, Vorsteveld, *Het joodse werkdorp in de Wieringermeer 1934–1941*, 122–3; Wasserstein, *The Ambiguity of Virtue*. 114–16.

On 11 June, the German police took about 300 men, mostly young German Jews, hostage as a reprisal for two resistance assaults in April and May. SS-men and Dutch police officers apprehended the men in their homes or temporary places of residence. They used different lists, including the one supplied by the Jewish Council and another that contained Max's name and address. The Germans didn't repeat the February *razzia*, possibly out of fear for a new strike, and this time they selected most of their victims from the less loved group of German Jews.

The SD gathered the young men at the new office of the *Aussenstelle* in Amsterdam-South. The already mentioned wartime pamphlet describes how Barbie was in command: 'He was drunk and walked jokingly along the rows of hostages. He took care that their number remained up and complete.'[39] Some of the boys were ill and allowed to go back home. The SD grabbed new hostages from the street. All of them were deported. Just like the men taken away in February, most were murdered in concentration camps.

Eventually, the responsibilities of the Jewish Council were extended, covering the whole of the Netherlands, and it became the instrument through which the Germans announced and executed their anti-Jewish measures. The Council and its policies also met resistance, which was expressed by clandestine papers such as *Het Parool*. An initial Jewish opponent was Herman Frijda, an economics professor at the University of Amsterdam, where he had been *Rector Magnificus* (chancellor) in 1938. He was well known in the resistance groups to which Nol and Ter belonged. They were also associated with his son Leo, who we'll meet later. The professor had been involved in the aid for refugees before the war. He refused to take a seat on the Jewish Council.[40]

The group of Nol and Ter in and around the Oosteinde Home decided to use opportunities offered by the Jewish Council. They utilised the positions and jobs that its members could occupy in the Council administration. For example, after the arrests on 11 June 1941, the group built a warning system for raids. When a German action was in preparation, the Council was usually informed and an associate in the Council office phoned Alice Heymann-David, the friend of Nol and Ter and one of the three group leaders, who as Secretary had access to the telephone in the Home. The group also used the phone in the home of Herman Frijda, because they knew the professor could be trusted. Following phone calls, other group members were warned through messengers, who mostly cycled or walked.[41]

The most publicly outspoken Jewish opponent of the Jewish Council was Lodewijk Visser, the former president of the Supreme Court – the highest

---

39. Pamphlet, 'Mauthausen, 1941'.
40. Presser, *Ondergang*, vol. I, 82. Interview A. Stertzenbach-David.
41. Interview A. Stertzenbach-David.

legal authority in the Netherlands. This opposition brought Visser in conflict with Cohen. He wrote to the chairman of the Council:

> It is possible that in the end the occupier will achieve his aim [in relation to the Jews], but it is our duty as Dutchmen and as Jews to do everything that will prevent him from achieving that aim, to refrain from anything that will pave the way for him.[42]

Visser was president of the Jewish Coordination Committee (JCC). It had been formed at the end of 1940. Cohen was also a member of the JCC, which contained a mixture of Zionists, representatives of religious congregations, an industrialist and a politician. The JCC aimed to unite the Jewish population in the Netherlands. For a short period under German occupation, the JCC was the dominant force among Dutch Jewry.[43] This position came to an end after the Germans formed the Jewish Council and the Council became responsible for the whole of the Netherlands

The conflict between Visser and Cohen, was in part about working with the German authorities. Cohen felt he had to listen to the occupiers and – sometimes under private protest – obey their orders, work with them and implement their decrees to avoid the Germans forcefully carrying out their measures.[44] Visser's guiding principle was that the Jews were Dutch citizens, who had the constitutional right to demand that the Dutch authorities would look after their interests and negotiate with the occupiers on their behalf. He wanted no direct contacts with the Germans, recognising only the Dutch authorities.

Visser protested publicly against persecution and deportation. Visser worked with the resistance paper *Het Parool*. His son, Ernst Lodewijk was a member of the group that produced and distributed the paper (he was arrested in July 1942 and murdered in Mauthausen). When Cohen on behalf of the Germans threatened Visser with deportation to a concentration camp if he would not end his actions, Visser replied on 14 February 1942 that he took note of the threat, but he didn't promise to sit still, adding to have been impressed by 'the humiliation that has been brought upon you, who knows the history of these actions'.[45] However, these were almost Visser's last words; he died three days later.

---

42. NIOD 248-1798a; Herzberg, *Kroniek der Jodenvervolging, 1940–1945*, 194; Melkman, 'De briefwisseling tussen Mr L.E. Visser en Prof. Dr. D. Cohen'. See also Herzberg, *Kroniek der Jodenvervolging*, 189–96; Michman, 'The Controversial Stand of the Joodse Raad in Holland', 9–68; Presser, *Ondergang*, vol. I, 82. Compare Gans, *Memorboek*, 755, 807; Kristel, *Geschiedschrijving als opdracht*, 173.
43. Michman, Beem, Michman, *Pinkas*, 174–86.
44. For a recent history of the Jewish Council, see Van der Boom, *De Politiek van het Kleinste Kwaad*.
45. Gans, *Memorboek*, 807.

As explained elsewhere,[46] the dispute between Visser and Cohen brings out how two well-integrated men from a similar background but with distinct personalities and life experiences made different choices. Visser took a principled, legal stand, which resulted in resistance, whereas Cohen chose a pragmatic cooperation course.

In short, this chapter shows how, in an atmosphere of general passive uneasiness during the first two years of occupation, German anti-Jewish measures and the acts of Dutch National Socialist brought about the incidence of specific forms of Jewish resistance, mostly from people who were directly affected. Acts of polemic and defensive resistance occurred across the Jewish population. Prominent figures in education, business and legal circles such as Leo Polak, Arnold Kahn and Lodewijk Visser raised public protests about the German decrees. Rabbis such as Simon de Vries and Philip Frank spoke out too. The student Henk van Gelderen took a small step towards resistance by refusing to register as a Jew. Working-class Jews fought on the street to defend their neighbourhood against National Socialist attacks. The leaders of this fightback were trained boxers and wrestlers, young men experienced in street brawls and those with strong political convictions, such as Lard Zilverberg. Property owners attempted to protect their premises, for example, Ernst Cahn, one of the proprietors of ice cream parlour Koco. Jewish workers took part in the general strike to protest against the *razzia* of February 1941.

The immediate consequences of resistance became clear in the spring of 1941. When caught, resisters faced death in front of a firing squad or in a camp such as Buchenwald and Mauthausen.

Leading figures in the Jewish population segment of the Netherlands were forced to make a strategic choice: pragmatic cooperation with the German occupiers to prevent the implementation of anti-Jewish measures by force, further *razzias* and other anti-Jewish violence; or opposition and resistance. David Cohen chose the first option and became one of the chairmen of the Jewish Council, appointed by the Germans. Herman Frijda refused a seat on the Council. Overt opposition to the Council came from Lodewijk Visser, motivated by legal principles and his life experience. His organisation, the JCC, could have become a central force in Jewish resistance in the Netherlands, but it was overshadowed by the Jewish Council, and disappeared with Visser's death. More covertly, some individuals decided to make use of their position or employment in the Jewish Council organisation to protect themselves and others against German *razzias* and actions.

---

46. Braber, *This Cannot Happen Here*, 35–6, 41, 54, 95, 107–10, 113–14, 156–8, 163. See also Polak, *Leven en werken van mr. L. E. Visser*; Schrijvers, *Rome, Athene, Jeruszalem*; Somers, *Voorzitter van de Joodse Raad*.

The care of Nol and Ter's Oosteinde group for illegal refugees, started before 1940, acquired a defensive resistance character; that's to say, work that was an attempt to prevent the National Socialists from reaching their goals. The group started to complement care work with other clandestine activities. But before these new shoots bore fruit, a big change occurred in the lives of Ter and Nol.

Chapter 4

THE BIRTH OF RUTH

Ruth, the first daughter of Nol and Ter, was born on 2 April 1941 in The Hague. We don't know why they gave her this Hebrew name, meaning friend, or why Ter went to The Hague for the delivery. The name suggests they were looking forward with joy to the child's arrival. There may have been various reasons why Ter left Amsterdam for the birth. Perhaps there was too much unrest in the capital. Ter's mother lived in The Hague and maybe Ter wanted her to be present at the delivery. Before the war, Ter had probably worked for a short while in this city as a nurse. She may have known a clinic or midwife who could assist with the birth. In any case, Ter and Ruth stayed for 10 days in The Hague, after which they came to the apartment on the Nieuwe Herengracht in Amsterdam.[1]

Just as the wedding, the birth was an occasion that usually makes people happy, but now it took place at a moment which otherwise offered little to celebrate. The German armed forces consolidated their success in Western Europe, despite the setback in the Battle of Britain. In South-East Europe their armies overran the Balkan and Greece. Germany and the Soviet Union still maintained their pact, which gave Hitler a free hand in the west and Poland and presented Stalin with the chance to occupy the Baltic states and the eastern part of Poland. The pact didn't come to an end until the Germans attacked the Soviets in June 1941. In December of that year, the United States of America was drawn into the war.

In the Netherlands, the Germans pressed ahead with the separation and isolation of the Jews from the rest of the population. The measures that were aimed to accomplish segregation, usually announced by the Jewish Council, were increasingly accompanied by *razzias*. These raids created fear and ensured widespread obedience. The Oosteinde Home became a part of the Council machine. The Oosteinde group member Max Rubinstein, for example, was appointed as youth leader, a low-paid position, but as we shall see, it offered advantages to the resistance group.

---

1. Interview T. Kolthoff.

Ruth's birth completely altered the daily life of Ter and Nol. Similar to many other households, maintaining the everyday routine in wartime had not been easy, but now it became much more difficult. The cost of living had risen by one-third since May 1940. Ter had no job, which kept the family income down. Not working wasn't unusual for a married woman. Many working women had lost their jobs during the economic depression of the 1930s. Long before the war, their families survived on a basic income. Ordinary people were often dependent on social security and this dependence was usually found to be humiliating. After May 1940 problems arose for everybody, but some people suffered more severely, notably when prices soared for electricity, gas, oil, coal and other fuel for heating and the preparation of warm food.[2]

On top of that hardship came the rationing of essential goods. During the first year of the German occupation bread, butter, meat, textiles, shoes, soap and tobacco were rationed. You were only able to buy a limited amount of food if you had obtained a registration card and distribution coupons. Because of the shortages, you had to queue for a long time or buy on the black market, if you could afford its prices. Many housewives used tricks from the 1930s crisis years to put something on the table. Ter learned what mums in poor families had known all along, for example, how to cut extra slices of bread from a loaf or whip up butter with water to cover more slices.

Caring for a baby proved arduous. There was a shortage of nappies and in Amsterdam it was almost impossible to buy a potty. We don't know whether Ter had one, but instead of using nappies she could put Ruth on a baby mat, a rubber sheet with holes through which fluids seeped into a tray and on which the baby without a nappy remained dry. You got these tips from other housewives or found them in women's magazines. As discussed elsewhere,[3] Jewish publications and rabbis also offered practical help and spiritual solace.

Despite having a new-born at home, Nol and Ter persisted in their decision to resist the Germans. However, major changes arose in their resistance work. Kurt and Jo, the German refugees who had moved in with them in June 1940, had produced an underground paper in their apartment. After a few months the two refugees found their own accommodation, but they returned to Nol and Ter's home to use the attic for typing articles and duplicating leaflets. They mostly covered news that they heard on the Allied radio and that they passed on to give people courage.

Kurt and Jo were not the only visitors. Nol and Ter also received people who were involved in armed resistance or were planning sabotage actions. Some of these persons came from their friend Trudel van Reemst-De Vries in

---

2. Beek, Scherphuis, 'Het dagelijks leven. De Vrouwen'; Walda, *Terug in de tijd*.
3. Braber, *This Cannot Happen Here*, 62, 83, 85–6, 92, 157.

Vlaardingen. Shortly after May 1940, Trudel had a visit from two men. They took Trudel's husband Theo for a walk along the river Meuse. Trudel never heard what they discussed, but she knew that the two men were Communists who had been instructed by their party to form military-style sabotage units.

Trudel's husband had been selected because he was a veteran of the Spanish Civil War. Men like him and former Dutch army conscripts were recruited for the sabotage groups. Through his professional contacts, Theo could lay his hands on chemicals and other materials that were needed to make bombs. Soon after the visit of the two functionaries, Trudel noticed that her husband started to collect explosive chemicals. The couple were then contacted by armed resistance groups, foremost those of Gerrit Kastein and Krijn Breur.

Kastein[4] was a medical doctor in The Hague. This restless and driven man had been born in 1909 in a small town in the east of the Netherlands and studied medicine in Groningen, Heidelberg and Leiden. He had married a German woman – they had a son and later a daughter. Gerrit had finished his studies, obtained his doctorate with the thesis *Eine Kritik der Ganzheitstheorien* and worked as a neurologist. Politically, he had first been a Revolutionary Socialist, then joined the Communist party, assisted refugees to escape from Germany and took part in the Spanish Civil War, where he treated wounded Republican soldiers. After that he had found a practice in The Hague for a Social Democratic health service. He was connected to several resistance groups and involved in a range of clandestine activities, determined on starting the armed struggle against the Germans as soon as possible.

Breur[5] was younger but no less impatient. This non-Jew had been born in 1917 in a small town in the province of South Holland. During his years at secondary school, Krijn had been an active Social Democrat and leading member of Socialist youth organisations – a friendly and good-humoured man but 'seriously anti-Fascist'.[6] He had served his time as an army conscript in the Netherlands before he went to Spain in 1937 to join the International Brigade. He was seriously wounded, but returned to the front after his recovery and was badly wounded again. He came back to the Netherlands in 1939, took up studying philosophy, was mobilised in August but discharged because of his Civil War injuries. He lost his Dutch citizenship as he had fought in Spain, and being stateless made it difficult for Krijn to find work and he wasn't entitled to social benefits. He tried his hand at journalism. In 1940 his girlfriend Aat got

---

4. De Jong, *Het Koninkrijk der Nederlanden in de Tweede Wereldoorlog*, vol. VI, 167; Galesloot, Legêne, *Partij in het verzet*, 31, 64, 108–10; Goudriaan, *Verzetsman Gerrit Kastein 1910–1943*.
5. Breur, *Een verborgen herinnering*; Breur, 'Krijn Breur'; Breur, *Een gesprek met mijn vader*; interview T. van Reemst-De Vries.
6. Interview T. van Reemst-De Vries.

pregnant. They were married, settled in Amsterdam and had a son and later a daughter.

In Spain Krijn had met Samuel 'Sally' Dormits.[7] Sally had been born in 1909 in Rotterdam, but unusually, spent part of his youth in Latin America. After this upbringing he had volunteered in 1937 for the Spanish Republican army. Back in the Netherlands, Sally started selling radio parts in The Hague. He was married to Annette Hartog and they had a son, Maurits, born in 1933. In 1941 Sally started resistance work. He tried to involve a large number of the men he had encountered in Spain. For this purpose, Sally compiled an extensive administration of their personal details. His resistance group was called the Dutch People's Militia. In 1941 local Militia groups were formed in Rotterdam, The Hague and Amsterdam, one of which consisted of employees of Hollandia-Kattenburg, a clothing factory in Amsterdam-North that produced garments for the German army.

Krijn was the link between Theo, Gerrit, Sally and Nol:

> [Krijn] was such a darling. He taught me how to shoot: 'Nol, pull the trigger now, you must do it now.' He was standing right in front of me. If I had done it, he'd have been killed. There was a bullet in the chamber. Together we made the first firebombs in my home.[8]

The groups used the self-made bombs to attack German munition depots and army garages. Ter, Trudel and other women such as their friend Juud Oostenbroek, the social work student who cared for illegal refugees of the Oosteinde group, now not only distributed food, but they also carried mysterious packages. With or without their knowledge, they were trafficking weapons and parts for bombs such as the chemicals from Theo and the electric parts that Sally could obtain. The packages also held clothes and falsified documents such as the identity cards that resistance members needed to escape detection and arrest. Finally, the couriers circulated underground papers and leaflets like the bulletins produced by Kurt and Jo.

The courier work ballooned quickly. Juud felt sometimes that the women were misused to transport less important items. She was furious when she discovered that a suitcase she had dragged all over town didn't contain underground materials but an expensive dinner set. Or when somebody asked her to take his suit to the cleaners. Okay, she thought, this man is unable to go

---

7. NIOD 248- 2068; De Jong, *Het Koninkrijk der Nederlanden in de Tweede Wereldoorlog*, vol. VI, 66, 70, 168–70, 172; Presser, *Ondergang*, vol. II, 17.
8. Interview A. Bueno de Mesquita.

outdoors. But later she was amazed to see him walking the street, completely at ease and smoking a cigarette:

> It was of course unavoidable in these exceptional circumstances, with all the accompanying tension and stress, that human weaknesses were exposed. But you struggled on. You continued because so many lives depended on you. You wouldn't even consider stopping after a quarrel or difficulties.[9]

Resistance groups often used women as couriers.[10] Apparently, the German and Dutch police suspected women less when they saw them on the street carrying packages. Later, after the introduction of labour conscription for men, it became even more difficult for males to act as couriers, because the police were constantly stopping them on the street and inspecting their papers to check whether the men were exempted from labour duty. Furthermore, females found it easier to hide weapons, explosives and other clandestine materials under their clothing or conceal them in shopping bags and prams. Nevertheless, when female couriers were caught, notably Jewish women, they could expect severe punishment, often resulting in death.

The first assaults and sabotage actions committed by the resistance groups to which Nol and Ter belonged took place in 1941 as the sky above the Jews in the Netherlands darkened. During the next year, the Germans started to prepare the deportation of the Jews from the Netherlands. Some of these preparations began with the German Jews who lived in the Netherlands. They lost their German citizenship. Their property was confiscated by the German state. They had to register with the *Zentralstelle für jüdische Auswanderung* (Central Office for Jewish Emigration) in Amsterdam-South. They had to complete long forms. Many panicked. Others sighed with relief – they were allowed to emigrate, weren't they?

However, fear mushroomed after German Jews were told that instead of emigration, they were to be sent to forced labour camps. Following implementation of this decree the National Socialists accelerated the evacuation of all Jews from small provincial towns and villages to Amsterdam. They had to find accommodation in designated neighbourhoods; the Germans didn't erect a ghetto, but they attempted to concentrate the Jews in parts of the Dutch capital.

In March 1942, German Jews were ordered to attach a Star of David on their front door. Two months later Jews in the Netherlands were forced

---

9. Interview J. Wolf-Oostenbroek.
10. Graaff, Marcus, *Kinderwagens en Korsetten*.

to wear a yellow star with the word 'Jew' displayed in the middle. It had to be sewn on their outer clothing. Not everybody complied. A teacher told his pupils that he wouldn't wear the star, because he didn't recognise the authority of the occupiers – he went into hiding and survived. How the group around the Oosteinde Home felt about the star is shown by the poem *The Mark*, written by a group member, Rosey Pool, about whom more will follow later. She wrote:

> I wore it like my skirt, like my shoes,
> Hardly feeling insult, hardly feeling spite
> Until I saw a child in the silent town,
> Where it walked alone with that yellow stain,
> Which soiled the child like stinking dung
> And that I had worn without hate all along.[11]

In summary, this period saw the continuation of symbolic and polemic Jewish resistance against an increasing number of anti-Jewish measures, including the introduction of the yellow star. It was contained in the clandestine papers produced by the political activists who had hidden with Ter and Nol. Via their friend Theo van Reemst, the couple was also engaged in offensive resistance, which was expressed through sabotage acts and assaults on the German military and their facilities. Krijn Breur formed the link between Ter and Nol and men like Gerrit Kastein and Sally Dormits. Some of the bombs they used were assembled in Ter and Nol's home. In offensive resistance, women had crucial functions, often as couriers who supplied the attackers with documents, arms and explosives. Overall, women often played a decisive role in resistance work, not only because of their ability to act as couriers, but also because they possessed the ingenuity, resilience and determination displayed by Ter, Trudel van Reemst-deVries and Juud Oostenbroek.

Although not directly connected, the intensification of the offensive resistance coincided with the German preparations of the expulsion of Jews from the Netherlands. German Jews, now stateless, were the first to be selected.

---

11. The poems by Rosey Pool in this book come from the manuscript of an unpublished biography, *The Marvellous Gift of Friendship* (Apeldoorn, 1986) by Anneke Schouten-Buys. The Jewish Historical Museum in Amsterdam holds a similar typescript. Anneke allowed me to transcribe some of the verses, which I have translated for this book. Rosey Pool produced several collections, including: *In Memoriam Matris*; *De Schaduw* and *Verzen 1943*.. See also Buys, 'Rosey E. Pool (1905–1971), Poet, Compiled Anthologies on African American Poetry, The Netherlands'; Geerlings, 'A Visual Analysis of Rosey E. Pool's Correspondence Archives'; Geerlings, 'Survivor, Agitator'; Schouten-Buys, 'Rosey E. Pool: An Appreciation'.

During the evacuation from the provinces, some of those who had lived in provincial towns and villages were sent to Westerbork. In October 1941 this former refugee camp in the eastern province of Drenthe, about 10 kilometres south of Assen, had been turned into a concentration camp. From July 1942, it became the main Dutch transit camp for the deportation of Jews.

Chapter 5

DEPORTATION

The first deportation train left the Netherlands in the night of 14 to 15 July 1942. Its destination was Auschwitz. By September 1943, more than 93,000 Jews had been taken from the Netherlands. This figure rose to about 107,000 in September 1944. Only a few thousand survived. Most of the others were gassed in the extermination camps of Auschwitz and Sobibor, often on arrival after a gruelling train journey in locked goods wagons or cattle carriages that lasted several days. The remaining victims died quickly, mostly of hunger and disease in slave labour camps.[1]

The German-Jewish friends of Nol and Ter belonged to the first group that was to be deported. In February 1942, the Jewish Council agreed with the planned transport of some 20,000 German and stateless Jews from the Netherlands to Poland. However, that wasn't enough for the Germans. At the end of June the Council was told that Dutch Jews would also be summoned for what was called *Arbeitseinsatz* (labour assignment) or the even more misleading Dutch term *werkverruiming* (increased employment) in eastern Europe.[2]

The National Socialists were planning the deportation in regular – sometimes weekly – transports of thousands of people, spreading the uprooting over time. About a hundred of these transports were foreseen. The *Zentralstelle* in Amsterdam-South sent out the deportation orders to each individual that was to be transported, first by mail, later the Dutch police delivered the notices. It was planned that those who were called up had to go to the office of the *Zentralstelle* to complete the required forms, and to hear when they would travel to the transit camp of Westerbork. However, sometimes they went straight from the *Zentralstelle* or another collection point to Westerbork or a different camp. From there they embarked on the journey to Poland.

This was a dark period for Nol and Ter. When the deportation from the Netherlands started, the news about the course of the war in general remained discouraging. The German armies had suffered a few military defeats, but

---

1. Herzberg, *Kroniek der Jodenvervolging, 1940–1945*, 134, 155–6; Presser, *Ondergang*, vol. I, 251.
2. Presser, *Ondergang*, vol. I, 246.

they were still able to launch large-scale offensives. In the Soviet Union, the Germans withdrew from Moscow, but they continued the siege of Leningrad and were on the attack in Stalingrad. In North Africa, the Germans and Italians had been pressed back, but an Allied victory still seemed impossible in the short term.

Did Nol and Ter know what awaited them if they were summoned for deportation and obeyed the order? In 1942, virtually nobody in the Netherlands knew what happened after *Auswanderung*[3] (emigration) to eastern Europe and what the 'labour assignment' there entailed – the language used by the Germans helped to hide their intentions. However, whatever you thought, it couldn't be good. The stories about the mass killings of Jews after the German invasions of Poland in 1939 and the Soviet Union in 1941 were well known. And now there were new reports. In May 1942, Nol and Ter read in a clandestine newspaper about 'the mass exile of Jews to destroyed areas of Poland. The Jewish part of the Dutch population will be exterminated in cold blood; men, women and children'.[4] Occasionally, from June 1942, news about the use of deadly poison gas was broadcasted on the Allied radio. At the end of 1942, the Allied governments accused Germany of the systematic extermination of the Jews in Europe. The 13-year-old Anne Frank, who listened clandestinely to Allied broadcasts, asked in her diary about the fate of the deported Jews: 'How will they live in faraway and barbarian areas?' She had already heard the answer to that question: 'We assume that most of them will be murdered. The English radio talks about gassing, which is probably the quickest way to die.'[5] However, despite news of mass murder, people who really didn't want to know could remain ignorant, or in any case, act as if they didn't know about the slaughter.

Nol and Ter knew something about what lay in store for the deportees, but like other Jews in the Netherlands they were unable to tell what deportation meant exactly.[6] Nevertheless, in July 1942 more than one-third of the total number of persons who were summoned for the first transport from Amsterdam didn't turn up. In other cities the disobedience was relatively greater.[7] Ignoring the deportation notice wasn't easy, because it meant disregarding the advice of the Jewish Council, which instructed people to obey. Actually, it was outright dangerous, because when you were caught disobeying a German order, you were threatened with being sent to notorious concentration camps such as Mauthausen, from where nobody seemed to return. When

---

3. Presser, *Ondergang*, vol. I, 7, 173.
4. *De Waarheid* 10 May 1942. See also Galesloot, Legêne, Morriën, *De Waarheid in de oorlog*, 120.
5. Barnouw, Stroom, *De Dagboeken van Anne Frank*, 291.
6. See also Van der Boom, '*Wij wisten niets van hun lot*'.
7. Michman, Beem, Michman, *Pinkas*, 511; Romijn, 'The War', 319.

despite the Council advice and the German threat, many didn't show up at the deportation centres, the Germans took hundreds of Jewish hostages as a reprisal. Later more and more Jews were rounded up in *razzias* on the streets or collected from their houses at night by Dutch policemen, including special units, who forcefully gathered many Jews from their homes.

Jews who were married to a non-Jew weren't to be deported, later only on the condition that they consented to be sterilised. Some specific groups were exempted from deportation and they received what the Germans called a *Sperre*. This included some occupations such as diamond cutters and individuals who were employed by the Jewish Council. The real value of the exemptions was unknown, until it transpired that they were only granted temporarily and could be revoked instantly.

For most Jews in the Netherlands it was difficult, if not impossible to extract themselves from deportation. You could flee, but neutral or Allied territory was far away and hard to reach. The Dutch landscape offered little cover as the flat countryside had no large forests or deserted areas. Going into hiding in the home of a non-Jew seemed the only plausible option. However, you needed an awful lot to go into hiding. For a start, a shelter. Often the first place was close to your home, in towns or cities, with friends or colleagues. When this hide-out became unsafe, you had to find another. And how long would that one last? Nobody was able to predict accurately the time you had to hide – weeks, months, years? Furthermore, you could only get food and other essential goods when you had official ration cards and coupons, but you no longer received these cards and coupons when you went into hiding. You might be able to buy food or ration documents, just as you could purchase falsified personal documents without the J, but they were usually expensive. Few Jews had the financial means to pay for it all. You could steal or falsify documents yourself, but who had the ready skills to do that properly? And finally, without these papers you couldn't go out on the street or travel by public transport because of frequent roadblocks and checks.

The problems grew infinitely worse for people like Ter and Nol who had children. There weren't enough hiding places, never mind shelters for families. Often, parents had to leave one of more of their children with non-Jewish helpers. That resulted in terrible dilemmas and questions you couldn't answer. Can you hand over your child? Will it be safe with people you don't know? How long will the child be secure with them? And after that? Would it be better to stay together and face fate? Similar issues arose with elderly parents and family members. It was simply impossible to take them with you when you went into hiding.

Plus, there was the constant danger of betrayal or of being discovered by accident, and then your punishment would be severe. Despite all the problems and risks, many Jews tried to hide. After the deportation started in July 1942, possibly about 28,000 Jews went into hiding in the Netherlands – one out of every five who were registered in 1941. Almost 12,000 of them were betrayed, discovered and deported, which illustrates the difficulties Jews in the Netherlands met when they tried to escape deportation.[8]

Non-Jews and Jews who were married to non-Jews were able to help as were people who were active in organised resistance. However, the general population wasn't geared up to assist high numbers of Jews going into hiding and most Jews didn't know people in the still small resistance groups. It wasn't until much later in the war that some groups grew to become large resistance organisations who looked after many people in hiding, such as the non-Jewish men who dodged the forced labour draft and often found shelter in remote buildings such as farms.

Many Jews in hiding were assisted and cared for by Jewish individuals and small Jewish rescue and care groups. One of them was Nol and Ter's group in and around the Oosteinde Home. Their care work was a continuation of the activity from before the war, when they looked after political refugees. Now this care was extended to more people and provided on a much more intense level, not only refugees and opponents of National Socialism, but also Jews who wanted to avoid deportation and needed almost daily help. The group was able to use the experience it had gained before May 1940, such as the need for secrecy and discipline or the usefulness of a tight group structure with lively young individuals who were prepared and able to move around and supply people in their hiding places.

The group also benefited from a new function of the Oosteinde Home, when the Jewish Council located there a department that was responsible for assisting persons who were to be deported. The Council advised people to obey the deportation order, but it wanted to equip them as best as possible for the transport and what was expected to await them in eastern Europe. For this purpose, the department in the Home collected and distributed items such as rucksacks and blankets. The leaders of Nol and Ter's group tried to get the department to recruit its members as employees, so that they got some protection from deportation in the form of a *Sperre* and their positions could be exploited, which became even more important when the Council started a workshop to repair collected items that were damaged or broken.

---

8. ARA: Centraal Archief Bijzondere Rechtspleging: W. Lages IIIb; NIOD 248–0998g and q; Croes, Tammes, *'Gif laten wij niet voortbestaan'*, 174–81; Houwink ten Cate, ' "Het Jongere Deel" '; De Jong, *Het Koninkrijk der Nederlanden in de Tweede Wereldoorlog*, vol. VI, 356–8; Sijes, *Studies over Jodenvervolging*, 141.

This workshop was opened in The Gallery, the arcade that had survived the Palace of People's Industry fire of 1929. The Gallery lay directly behind the Oosteinde Home and could be reached through a passage just past the Home building on number 24. It had been a shopping mall with beautifully windowed and meticulously decorated retail outlets, which sold fashion and luxury items such as cigars and hand-made pottery. After the destruction of the Palace, their business declined when the footfall from Palace visitors vanished and the inhabitants of the surrounding neighbourhood could no longer afford the high prices charged by The Gallery stores. Just a few shops remained, but they didn't flourish. So there was plenty of space in The Gallery.

The Jewish Council installed the workshop at number 4 in The Gallery. The group of Ter and Nol decided to fit out this workshop and the two buildings of the Home on the Oosteinde for their own purposes. They constructed double walls and floors, so that they could hide people, materials, documents and money. For example, behind a cupboard in the Home they built a space where 10 persons could hide. The attic of the workshop in The Gallery was also turned into a shelter for people in hiding.

Group members who worked for the Jewish Council received permits with which they were allowed to go out at night, that is after eight o'clock when the curfew started. The group started copying these permits, which became their first forged documents. Nol and Ter's friend Max Rubinstein, who had been involved in the care for refugees, excelled in the counterfeit work. The forging improved constantly: 'First we had fake identity cards. They were poor imitations. We then also received stolen documents that we could adapt. We stole them from the registry offices.'[9] Later some group members received 'real' documents, such as identity and ration cards. These were better, because the numbers of stolen personal documents such as ration cards were blocked by the authorities and no more coupons were issued for these cards.

What were 'real' documents and how did the group get them? Two young German Jews in Amsterdam, Marga Grünberg and her brother Manfred,[10] had been involved in some of the pre-war activity in the Oosteinde Home. Max Rubinstein had briefly been hiding in their home. After the start of the deportation, Marga established a contact with a person who worked in the offices in the Amsterdam population register. This person was able to provide them with new identity cards that were not marked with a J. They passed

---

9. Interview M. Rubinstein and U. Rubinstein-Littmann.
10. Interviews M. Grünberg and M. Grünberg, and L. Weil. See also CVA 17028 and 'Zonder "J" in mijn persoonsbewijs had ik mijn vrijheid terug' (https://www.verhalenoverdeoorlog.nl/nl/interviews/marga-grunberg).

some of them on to their friends in the Home and several Palestine Pioneers (see below).

In addition, Uschi Littmann, the girlfriend of Max Rubinstein, knew a man who worked in the Amsterdam police headquarters, being in charge of the department that dealt with lost personal documents. He could be trusted. Uschi told the man when a group member would come to him to report a 'lost' document, for instance an identity card. The policeman noted their details, if necessary, under a false name. He in turn knew a man in the registry office. This civil servant inserted a card into the register with the information that the policeman provided. Then the registry produced a new identity card, but without a J, so that the Jewishness of the card holder was hidden. With the identity card a ration card and coupons could be obtained.

In this way, several group members received new identities and personal documents. Uschi Littmann, for example, became Ursula Maria Szèkely from Gutweiss in Czechoslovakia, an identity that fitted her dark hair and foreign accent. Ter was told to report at a pre-arranged time in a municipal office: 'I had to say that I was Greet van der Hoek. And that I had lost my papers. The man behind the window looked at me and said: "I see, you don't look Jewish at all."'[11] Ter got a new identity and personal documents, which enabled her to continue working as a resistance courier. The group also found a new source for falsified personal documents in An de Lange, a member of the TD group, a resistance organisation that specialised in this work, who had befriended the Oosteinde group leader Nathan Notowicz.[12]

Couriers like Ter were badly needed because the group had to care for a quickly growing number of people in hiding, who had to be supplied with food, forged documents, money, underground bulletins and news from family and friends. In July 1942, one of the couriers who worked with Ter and Nol, Juud Oostenbroek, helped her boyfriend Hans Wolf find a hiding place: 'After that I was inundated with requests from others.' Juud often had to care for the persons she helped to find a shelter. As the war progressed the anticipated period in hiding grew longer, for example: 'I asked a friend if somebody could stay overnight in her apartment. That night turned into a year and a half.'[13]

Ter and Nol and their friends in and around the Oosteinde Home didn't form the only rescue and care group that almost exclusively consisted of Jews. Another group was set up by Palestine Pioneers. It was probably no coincidence that this group used the same contacts at the Amsterdam police and the registry office to obtain personal documents, as there were links between

---

11. Interview T. Kolthoff.
12. Interview A. Notowicz-De Lange.
13. Interview J. Wolf-Oostenbroek.

the Oosteinde group and the Pioneers.[14] In addition, one of the Pioneers, Lilly Kettner (born in 1923 in Vienna),[15] worked with Walter Süskind in a collection centre in Amsterdam, where she witnessed the rescue of children (described later). What sets it apart from the Oosteinde group is that the Pioneers extended their activity of rescue and caring for people in hiding to helping their members escape to neutral or Allied territory.

The Pioneers were young Jews who had been preparing for emigration to Palestine. At the start of the occupation just over 800 Pioneers were living in several locations in the Netherlands, including New Gate in the Wieringermeer polder and a pavilion called Loosdrechtsche Rade near the small town of Loosdrecht, some 30 kilometres south-east of Amsterdam. The chances of emigration to Palestine – the purpose of their training – disappeared during the early years of the war. Nevertheless, preparation for future settlement in Palestine was continued.

Among the Pioneers, discussions took place about how to react to the deportations. Some felt that they shouldn't try to hide but endure the suffering for religious and historical reasons. Others argued they had to try and flee to Palestine. An initiative for building a clandestine organisation that helped Pioneers to escape was taken by youth leaders in Loosdrecht, such as Menachem Pinkhof and Joachim Simon. It came about at the start of the deportations in 1942, but the plans may have been made earlier – as mentioned before, in 1941 the Germans had unexpectedly cleared the Pioneer centre in the Wieringermeer and this may have caused the planning in Loosdrecht. In the summer of 1942 it also appeared that some of the Pioneers in Loosdrecht were making individual plans to get away. The leaders decided to create a set-up whereby all Pioneers would be able to go into hiding.[16]

To organise hiding places, the Pioneers had to rely on outside help. The Jewish Waterman family lived next to the Loosdrecht centre. Their daughter Mirjam, became Menachem Pinkhof's girlfriend and joined the initiative to prevent the deportation of Pioneers. She had worked in a children's institution

---

14. Interviews J. Reutlinger and G. Laske.
15. Brasz, Daams Czn, Ofek, Keny, Pinkhof, *De jeugdalijah van het Paviljoen Loosdrechtsche Rade 1940–1945*, 71.
16. NIOD 249-0296a, 1283. See also Brasz, Daams Czn, Ofek, Keny, Pinkhof, *De jeugdalijah van het Paviljoen Loosdrechtsche Rade 1940–1945*; Schippers, *De Westerweelgroep en de Palestinapioniers*; Regenhardt, Groot, *Om nooit te vergeten*. Other secondary sources are Avni, 'Zionist Underground in Holland and France and the Escape to Spain'; De Jong, *Het Koninkrijk der Nederlanden in de Tweede Wereldoorlog*, vol. VI, 354–6; Jakob, Van der Voort, *Anne Frank war nicht allein*, 169–81; Herzberg, *Kroniek der Jodenvervolging, 1940–1945*, 227–30, 270; Presser, *Ondergang*, vol. I, 448–51, vol. II, 12–16; Stegeman, Vorsteveld, *Het joodse werkdorp in de Wieringermeer 1934–1941*.

in nearby Bilthoven. One of her ex-colleagues was Joop Westerweel, not Jewish but a charismatic non-conformist and Socialist.[17] He was able to find hiding places in surrounding towns and villages and eventually the group was called after him.

As Pioneers from different centres were looking for ways to hide and escape, more people learned about the plans of the Westerweel group and the national Pioneer office in Amsterdam became a centre of clandestine activity. In this way, different units came into being next to the Westerweel group, but they collaborated on aspects of their work. In August 1942 friends in Amsterdam warned the group in Loosdrecht that the Germans intended to raid their centre. Within a few days the Pioneers went to their hiding places. After some months the group started to investigate an escape route to Allied territory. For this purpose, Joachim Simon, his wife Adina van Coevorden and two other Pioneers travelled to France. Joachim was able to make some useful contacts and returned to the Netherlands to set up the route after his wife and the two other Pioneers crossed the Swiss border.

Joachim 'Shushu' Simon was a refugee from Germany. He had been born in 1919 in Berlin. His mother had died shortly after his birth and for a year he was looked after by an aunt in Frankfurt. Back in Berlin, Shushu had visited a Jewish primary school and studied at a general gymnasium. His father had remarried in 1932 and Shushu moved again to his aunt in Frankfurt. After his father's death in 1935 Shushu had returned to Berlin with his aunt, and he finished his secondary education. In the summer of 1937 Shushu had joined the Palestine Pioneers in Germany. He was rounded up during the Kristallnacht in November 1938 and sent to Buchenwald. Following his release from that camp, Shushu moved to the Netherlands. To continue his Pioneer training, he worked on a Dutch farm. The physical labour couldn't have been easy for the young man, because Shushu suffered from asthma. In his spare time, he continued to study, borrowing books in Amsterdam. After May 1940 Shushu was appointed youth leader in Loosdrecht and became an active member of the national Pioneer organisation.

Shushu personified the tenacity of the Pioneers. This resolve was also a recurring theme in the letters he wrote to inspire others to be equally determined to succeed. On 20 November 1942 Shushu wrote in a letter to a friend in a concentration camp:

> When I think about you, being incarcerated, I'm grateful that I can be active. I still have the opportunity to try – and that's most important for us. It's still possible to fight against fate – even if we'll lose. And if I have

---

17. Schippers, 'The Palestine Pioneers and the Westerweel Group', 131.

an accident tomorrow, I can have peace. I'll not regret for one moment what I've done. We had the courage to fight and if we failed, that is our fate. And the thought that we haven't fought only for ourselves gives us courage.[18]

Shushu struggled with what he saw as his shortcomings. At times, he found himself too impatient, wanting quick results. When he wrote about this, the escape work wasn't yet well-organised and time was pressing. Shushu and the others had to make far-reaching decisions, while conducting a discussion with those who didn't want to go into hiding, often because they felt protected through the exemptions issued to them by the Jewish Council. Shortly before or in January 1943, Shushu wrote about this discussion to another friend:

> If we had a meeting now [...], would I not be forced to say [...] that on the basis of deductive, logical observation of the general situation [...] that this and this are our options and that our logical reaction should be so and not any different, that's to say, not await our fate as cattle that is being taken to the slaughter? Should I not demand action from everybody [...], especially as I feel this burdensome responsibility?!!!![19]

Shushu travelled several times to France to organise the escape network, but he was arrested. It is presumed that in captivity he killed himself on 27 January 1943.

Menachem Pinkhof and Mirjam Waterman took over Simon's role. Some Pioneers settled along the escape route and the Westerweel group was able to build a large organisation that helped Pioneers to escape in groups of two or three persons. After the summer of 1943, the number of escapees rose, including Pioneers who had managed to get out of Westerbork; about 25 were able to escape deportation from the transit camp. Following Shushu's death, the group had several more setbacks. Mirjam and Menachem were captured and ended up in Bergen Belsen. Joop Westerweel was arrested in March 1944; he was executed five months later. In the spring of 1944, the Germans destroyed the Pioneer organisation in Paris and several Pioneers in the Netherlands fell into German hands. In France Kurt Reitlinger took over the group's contacts with French Zionists and armed Jewish resistance

---

18. NIOD 249-1283. This folder contains a manuscript by Kochba (Adina van Coevorden) and Klinov, which incorporates this and the January 1943 letter (quoted below). According to the *Nieuw Israëlitisch Weekblad* 21 June 1987, this manuscript has been published in Hebrew under the title *Hamachteret Hachalutsith BeHolland Hekevoesa*.
19. NIOD 249-1283.

fighters. The Pioneers had also been able to obtain false identity papers that gave people the position of construction workers. At one point about 20 persons from the Pioneer organisation were working under this disguise on the Atlantic Wall in the Calais region.[20]

In total, the Westerweel group looked after well over 200 Pioneers. About 150 of them undertook the journey to Spain, 80 reached that country and 70 of them managed to settle in Palestine. Of the total of 820 Palestine Pioneers in the Netherlands at the start of the war, just over 400 went into hiding and 393 survived the war.[21]

Meanwhile, the Oosteinde Home group was lucky when Juud Oostenbroek met a civil servant who worked in the distribution office. She could make appointments to see him, and on these occasions collect rationing coupons for people in hiding. Their own coupons were blocked, so that these people would get caught if they came to the office and presented their ration cards. But Juud's civil servant turned a blind eye and she received the coupons. Once a week Juud took them to the Oosteinde Home, where Nathan Notowicz received them, always remaining 'silent'.[22]

That he was unable to thank Juud may have been part of Notto's personality, but it was also an illustration of the discipline and secrecy that the group maintained. The three group leaders – Nathan Notowicz, Alice Heymann-David and Ernst Levy – enforced a strict rule. Alice, for example, was known as 'Ali with the firm hand'.[23] The leaders also distinguished their treatment of what they regarded as important persons and ordinary group members. The young Polish Jew Sera Anstadt, who has been quoted earlier about the group's discipline, noticed this when she was summoned to come and see a woman she called 'Hanna', a leading German Communist. She later wrote about this episode:

> Hanna was always very severe and I was nervous in her presence. When I came into her room that afternoon there was another important functionary. I knew him well; he was the brother of a boy with whom I had been friendly for a while. But he had never uttered a word to me.

The functionary was Notto. Sera called him Otto:

> 'Sera,' started Hanna, 'I've asked you to come here to discuss a serious matter.' Her voice didn't sound as calm as I was used to. 'Otto needs a

---

20. Moore, *Victims and Survivors*, 168.
21. Schippers, 'The Palestine Pioneers and the Westerweel Group', 132–3.
22. Interview J. Wolf-Oostenbroek.
23. Interview M. Rubinstein and U. Rubinstein-Littmann.

place to hide. I've heard that you have a good place. Is that so?' 'Yes,' I said and assumed that she wanted to know who my contact person was for this hiding place. But she didn't mean that. 'Otto needs your hiding place. It's necessary,' she said. 'O,' I answered, frightened. 'I only got the address of the place, but I cannot reach the contact person. Where should I then go?' 'The only thing that matters is that Otto gets your place,' she stressed and remained silent after that.[24]

The demand was incontestable. Sera had to do what was regarded as her duty. Notto was an important party official. If Sera refused, she would be excommunicated. Then she could no longer expect any help from the group. So, Sera went with Notto and gave him the address of her hiding place.

Sera slept in the Oosteinde Home. Despite the discipline and secrecy, people talked about the group. It became known that Ter and Nol were able to get individuals exempted from deportation. This attracted people and the group grew quickly. Some came to ask for help, others offered assistance. Somebody had been able to obtain a stamp the Germans used, another copied it. Someone said he knew people who had food, others went the next day to collect it. All in all, this created a heated atmosphere in the Oosteinde Home. Although most group members still worked during the day, they no longer slept in their own house, especially after the German and Dutch police started to round up Jews for deportation from their homes in the evening and at night during the curfew.

By hiding in the Home, the group members avoided being collected from their houses. However, occasionally somebody was grabbed in the street, for example, a family member or an associate. How could the group try and rescue these people?

A young man named Jacques van de Kar[25] offered a solution. He had been born in 1917 in Amsterdam. His father had worked on the market. When their home had become too small, the family moved to Amsterdam-North. In 1934, they had returned to the city centre, four years later Jacques' mother died. The sport-loving and tall Jacques had started work in the North. His first job had been a delivery boy for a Jewish baker, but he didn't want to work on Sundays when his friends were off, so he moved on to a non-Jewish baker. After that Jacques worked for a manufacturer of suitcases and was an active trade union member. His older brother Jules was a Communist. Jacques was mobilised in 1939. He started resistance work with Jules; both took part in the

---

24. Anstadt, *Een eigen plek*, 69–70.
25. Van de Kar, *Joods Verzet*, 50–72.

street fighting in February 1941 and the general strike that followed the *razzia* in that month. Jacques then went into hiding for a while, because the Germans were looking for strike organisers – Jules was arrested (he died in Auschwitz in September 1942).

Jacques was summoned for deportation in July 1942. He was exempted, possibly because he was married and the breadwinner of the family. In any case, Jacques successfully applied to the Jewish Council for a job as messenger. Quickly after that he started rescuing people from deportation centres. This began in the *Expositur*, a section of the Jewish Council that liaised with the *Zentralstelle*.[26] As an employee of the Council, Jacques had access to deportation centres. He helped people escape after they had been gathered there. It mostly concerned individuals, including relatives, friends, associates and members of the Oosteinde group, who had been caught.

When somebody was picked up and the group wanted to free this person, they phoned the office where Jacques worked as a messenger. A meeting was set up in 213 Nieuwe Herengracht, where Jacques had recently found an apartment, only about 400 metres from where Nol and Ter lived. The group leader Ernst Levy taught Jacques that if somebody rang the bell at the agreed time, he shouldn't open straightaway but wait until the caller whistled the first five notes of the Yiddish song *Bei Mir Bistu Shein*. Then the coast was clear. Jacques let the visitor in and heard who was to be rescued. He went to the *Zentralstelle* and added their names to the lists of people who were allowed to leave because they had been exempted from deportation. Or he simply took people out, telling the guard that they were exempted. He also hid people in his carrier tricycle and a delivery truck. Sometimes he took them to his apartment, where they learned the address of their hiding place or he sent them to associates who could find a shelter.

The German occupiers also used the Dutch Theatre in the Plantation District as a collection centre for the deportation of Jews from Amsterdam. Across the avenue was a nursery for children whose parents awaited transport in the Theatre. Walter Süskind[27] worked in the Theatre and its nursery. Walter

---

26. NIOD 248-0998g.
27. NIOD 249-0364b/22; De Jong, *Het Koninkrijk der Nederlanden in de Tweede Wereldoorlog*, vol. VI, 258–9, 352–3, vol. VII, 310, 382; Van de Kar, *Joods verzet*, 50–69; Presser, *Ondergang*, vol. I, 343, 466; Roegholt, Wiedeman, *Walter Suskind and a Theatre in Holland*; Roegholt, Wiedeman, *Walter Süskind en de Hollandse Schouwburg*; Schellekens, 'Op zoek naar Walter Süskind'; Schellekens, *Walter Süskind*. See also *Secret courage. The story of Walter Suskind and the Jewish children of Amsterdam*, a 2005 film by Tim Morse, Karen Morse, Federico Muchnik and Ries Vanderpol (Morse Photography/M & M Films).

had been born in 1906 in Ludenscheid in Germany. He had been a margarine factory manager, who fled Germany in 1938 and lived from 1942 in Amsterdam. The Jewish Council appointed him as a manager in the Theatre. However, this spirited organiser used his position, knowledge of German and subtle ways of handling German officials to develop an initiative for smuggling children out of the deportation centre.

Adults awaiting deportation were unable to leave the Theatre complex, but babies, toddlers and young children were taken daily to the nursery. Walter's collaborators asked the parents whether they wanted their child to be rescued. The question was asked because the rescued children would disappear and Walter wanted to prevent parents from panicking when their child was suddenly gone. Following parental approval, Walter's co-workers[28] removed the registration documents of the children from the Theatre administration. Then they took the children over a path through the back gardens of the two houses next to the nursery to a Protestant school, where members of general resistance groups collected the children and took them to foster parents. Sometimes children were transferred on the street when Walter's collaborators had permission to take them for a group walk in the neighbourhood. In this manner hundreds of children were extracted from deportation. Walter himself couldn't or didn't want to go into hiding. He and his family went on transport towards the end of the deportations and died in camps and on death marches, which the National Socialists started after their evacuation of the camps during the advance of the Soviet armies.

Soon after the Theatre had become a deportation centre, Walter found Jacques van de Kar a post in the building. Jacques then formed his own team for rescue efforts. They also assisted people in escaping from the deportation trains, which left from a railway yard in the eastern harbour area of Amsterdam. The Oosteinde group arranged a pass for its member Max Rubinstein, which enabled him to enter the Theatre: 'I worked there with Jacques. I was actually his deputy.'[29] They usually helped detainees escape via the nursery or they hid people in the attic of the Theatre, after which Jacques and his helpers smuggled them out via an emergency exit at the side of the building. Sometimes they called an ambulance to take people away. Max was involved in about 40 escape attempts.

The group also had keys with which they could open the carriages of the deportation trains. They gave the keys to people on the train, so that they

---

28. See also M. Arian and B.-J. Film, 'Het Joodse verzet in en om de Hollandse Schouwburg', *Nieuw Israëlietisch Weekblad*, 12 March 1993.
29. Interview M. Rubinstein and U. Rubinstein-Littmann.

could open the door and jump from the train once it left the station and slowed down.

Furthermore, they stole armbands worn by employees of the Jewish Council, which were produced in a sewing workshop in the Oosteinde Home. Max Rubinstein's girlfriend, Uschi Littmann, worked there and every once and a while she could pinch some of the armbands. Max used them. During *razzias*, employees of the Council had to help on the deportation railway yard. They wore these armbands. Max gave them to people who were boarding the train, so that they could put them on their arm, act as if they were Council employees, disembark and walk off the railway yard. That went well until the Germans abolished the exemption symbolised by the armbands.

Max was rounded up from a street in a cordoned off area during one of the last large raids in Amsterdam. He was forced onto a tram, which took the prisoners to the railway yard. There he had to board the deportation train. He met a friend who was involved in the rescue work:

> We simply alighted the train. On the platform we took two suitcases that had been left there. We attached the armbands and acted as if we were innocently working there for the Council. The Germans were always quickly impressed when somebody wore a uniform or an official mark. They just let us go. We walked out of the railway yard and took the tram that went in the opposite direction. That is how we got out of the closed-off area.[30]

After Sera Anstadt had lost her hiding place, she and her younger sister Selma got a new shelter across the street from Max and Uschi in Amsterdam-South. Sera had received the information about this address from a woman who later turned out to have betrayed numerous people in hiding to the National Socialists. One morning the police arrived at the address and took Sera and Selma away. Uschi was warned and she asked Max to go and get the girls out of the transport train, but he was unable to act, because the woman across the street could also have betrayed him and his cover may have been blown.

However, by coincidence later that day one of the group's couriers, Juud Oostenbroek, went to Sera's hiding place to deliver food. The traitor opened the door and said: 'Something terrible has happened. There has been a raid, but I managed to send [Sera and Selma] to another safe house by a pony taxi.'[31] Juud didn't reply but walked away quickly – she simply didn't believe the woman. In the Oosteinde Home she heard that the girls had been taken.

---

30. Interview M. Rubinstein and U. Rubinstein-Littmann.
31. Interview J. Wolf-Oostenbroek.

Another friend from the Home was engaged to help Sera escape from the deportation area. Sera called him 'Tjoem':

> We went to a truck. There I was kissed effusively and congratulated by a big blond man. 'Where is Selma?' I asked. 'We couldn't help her,' said Tjoem. I looked from Tjoem to the blond man and then again to Tjoem. It was getting very quiet.

Sera felt ashamed. She started crying silently.

> The blond man moved me next to him in the truck, kissed me again, took my hand and I felt a large erection. I didn't say anything. I was incapable and let my hand rest again in my lap. He took my hand another time, now almost angrily and quickly got rid of his erection. We didn't say anything to each other.[32]

Suffering the sexual abuse, Sera had been saved, but Selma was deported and died.

Meanwhile, Max and Uschi were married in 1943 at a Jewish registry office: 'After the ceremony we both went to our work. At night we saw each other again in the hiding place.' Max met his parents regularly, but he was unable to save them: 'They knew that I was in the resistance. I offered to help them go into hiding, but they didn't want that. Like many other people, my parents underestimated what was going on.'[33]

The parents of Floor Przyrowski, the shy girl who had come to the Oosteinde Home, wanted very much that their daughter went into hiding, but like Max's parents they didn't want that for themselves. At first, they couldn't find a shelter for Floor, but the girl persisted: 'I'm not going to let them grab me.'[34] Group leader Ernst Levy, in the meantime married to Floor's sister Bella, promised that if she really wanted to go into hiding, he'd be able to fix it. And he did. Initially, Floor slept with Ernst and Bella in their hiding place. In the morning they walked from the shelter to the house of Ernst and Bella on one of the Amsterdam canals to get washed and changed for their daily work.

That went well until the German police in Düsseldorf started to investigate Ernst. His name had been mentioned by a man who was arrested in Germany. One morning, Floor, Bella and Ernst had just arrived home when Dutch policemen rang the doorbell. Floor saw what happened:

---

32. Anstadt, *Een eigen plek*, 97–8.
33. Interview M. Rubinstein and U. Rubinstein-Littmann.
34. Interview F. Brandon-Przyrowski.

They came to collect Ernst. I cannot remember exactly what I did, but I must have said something along the lines of 'I must go to school now.' They let me go. I ran to friends of Ernst. They told me I had to follow them. Walking away, I saw Ernst and Bella board a tram at the corner of the canal.[35]

Ernst and Bella were taken to the prison of Scheveningen, where the Germans kept people suspected of resistance work who could be questioned in nearby The Hague by German police units, which investigated clandestine activities across the Netherlands.

Floor, now back with her parents, was summoned for deportation. Did she obey because she had lost her hiding place? 'I went to have a look at the place where the people were gathered for deportation, but I was determined to go into hiding.' Desperate, she approached members of the Oosteinde group: 'I was sixteen but looked like fourteen. They gave me documents of somebody who was older. I only looked older when I wore lipstick.'[36] Somebody took her away on a bike. They cycled to an address in Amsterdam-West, a shelter that Ernst had kept for himself. She stayed there a long time, traumatised and deserted. Her parents were deported.

Ter was unable to save her mother from deportation. Cis Kolthoff had moved to another address in The Hague after her husband died. That address was in an upmarket neighbourhood. She had a ground floor flat with a room for a maid. Ter's mother refused to go into hiding. When she was collected from her home for transport in January 1943, Cis walked to the bathroom, where she tried to drink a potion. What this concoction was, we don't know, but she fell to the floor, was carried off and deported via Westerbork to Auschwitz, where she died.[37]

Ter and Nol themselves had a narrow escape. They were also involved in several armed resistance groups, including the Dutch People's Militia set up by Sally Dormits,[38] and that tie proved nearly fatal for the couple when the German police started rounding up Militia members. Krijn Breur helped Nol and Ter avoid arrest. That went as follows.

---

35. Interview F. Brandon-Przyrowski.
36. Interview F. Brandon-Przyrowski.
37. The journalist Jet Mok, granddaughter of Ter, made in 2013 a series of short radio documentaries about the war experiences of her grandmother. This information comes from these broadcasts.
38. NIOD 248-2068; De Jong, *Het Koninkrijk der Nederlanden in de Tweede Wereldoorlog*, vol. V, 824, vol. VI, 66, 70, 168–74. See also Van der Paauw, *Guerrilla in Rotterdam*.

In the summer of 1942, Sally conducted several assaults and sabotage actions, including attacks on trains and railway lines. For example, the Militia planted a bomb under a train that was scheduled to take German soldiers on leave from Rotterdam. The attack failed when a passing railway employee by accident touched the detonator switch; the device exploded but not the bomb itself. The employee, however, was killed. If successful, the attack would have caused numerous German casualties, which drew the attention of the German police. Sally was identified when he or a friend had to leave a bicycle during an attack in The Hague. The bike was registered in Sally's name. This led the police to his home address. The occupants weren't at home, but the officers found bomb-making equipment and explosive materials, internal reports on attacks and member lists of the Militia.

Sally, already divorced from Anette, became reckless. Following the firebombing of a German army depot in The Hague, he was arrested on 17 October 1942 for the attempted theft of a lady's purse, probably to steal an identity card without a J for his ex-wife, new girlfriend or a female Militia member. When they tried to search him in the police station, Sally drew a gun and shot himself through the head.

The lists found in Sally's home triggered widespread arrests among people with Militia connections. Within the framework of the anti-Militia action the German and Dutch police caught about 600 persons. Arrests of Militia suspects were also made at Hollandia-Kattenburg in Amsterdam. After the interrogation of a female employee, the German police rounded up all Jewish employees of the factory. Together with their families they were immediately deported.

When Krijn Breur heard about the arrest and death of Sally, he collected Sally's son and former wife and took them to Amsterdam. Krijn also came to warn Nol, because he was a member of the group, but at this stage Krijn felt that Nol and Ter didn't yet have to go into hiding. Instead, he told them to be extra careful, notably after Sally's sister and her husband came to shelter in their home. Problems started when Sally's sister was arrested when her identity documents were checked at a roadblock. This caused a police search of Ter and Nol's home, but they 'had everything worked out'.[39]

What happened? Nathan Notowicz had instructed Nol to build a hiding place in their home, where they could store clandestine materials. When the rounding up of Jews started, they also hid in this shelter. The raids always started at half past seven at night, so by seven Nol, Ter, Ruth and Nol's mother were in the hide-away. They heard Jews being taken away next door: 'Elderly people, eighty years of age. Children. Not taken by Germans. No, these people

---

39. Interview A. Bueno de Mesquita.

were dragged from their homes by Dutchmen. They screamed. At five past eight it was all over. You could set your watch by their timing.'[40]

Nol and Ter also had a daytime warning system in their home. Behind the front door, next to the meter cupboard, was a bell. If they had unexpected visitors, Nol's mother would open but ring the bell before she opened the front door, so that Ter and Nol could hide themselves and anything incriminating. Nol explained the system failed when Sally's sister was arrested and the police knocked their door:

> What did these rotters do? They kept hidden until the front door was opened, and then they burst in. What did my mother do? A remarkable woman. She was small, but she blocked the stairs and shouted: 'Hey! Hey, gentlemen, can you not raise your hat for an old woman?' The men obeyed and doffed their headgear. We heard that and hid everything. The clandestine papers and the resistance materials. Only the nursery room was full of stuff. They searched the whole house, apart from the nursery. We were told to 'clear that pigsty first'.[41]

The reason why the police didn't thoroughly search the house was probably because they hadn't come for Nol and Ter, but for Sally's brother-in-law. He was taken away. But what should Ter and Nol do now? At first, their group gave them the impression that they could remain at home, but after 10 days Krijn returned to alert Nol again:

> 'Nol, you and Ter need to get out of here, but you need to get out at once – we've been betrayed.' We showed them a clean pair of heels. My mother also went into hiding. She was a very realistic woman. For a while we lost touch with her, but she survived the war. My brother was gassed.[42]

After Krijn's second warning Nol and Ter hid in the shelter above The Gallery workshop behind the Oosteinde Home.

However, they couldn't take Ruth with them. She was one and a half years old, and the shelter had no facilities for a toddler. Nol and Ter also believed that taking Ruth with them was too dangerous. There was a constant danger that the Germans would trace them to the hiding place and they didn't want Ruth to be taken as a child of resistance people, if they couldn't avoid arrest.

---

40. Interview A. Bueno de Mesquita.
41. Interview A. Bueno de Mesquita.
42. Interview A. Bueno de Mesquita.

So Ruth had to go to foster parents. But who could rear her? A friend came to the rescue. This was Olga, one of Ter's former nursing colleagues. She was married to Wim Vasbinder, a doctor who had just been offered a general practice in Gramsbergen, a small town in the east of the Netherlands, near the German border. Ter asked Olga: 'Can you take care of Ruth?'[43] After all, nobody in Gramsbergen knew the couple and whether they had children, and Ruth would be safe there. Olga and Wim accepted Ruth and promised to care for her as long as it would take.

Krijn Breur was arrested on 19 November 1942 in The Hague. His wife Aat was also taken into custody. She was sent to the prison in Scheveningen with her second-born child, still a baby, but eventually the children of Krijn and Aat were taken in by her parents. Krijn was executed on 5 February 1943. Aat was transported to Ravensbrück, a concentration camp for females.[44]

Arrests were also made in Vlaardingen. Trudel van Reemst-De Vries was prepared, but couldn't prevent it when she and her husband Theo were taken prisoner. Trudel now also had a child, 10 months earlier she had given birth to a boy. She had taken into account that they may have to go into hiding, and she had agreed with friends in The Hague that they would nurse the child if anything happened to her. As the police was taking Trudel and Theo from their home, she was allowed to make a phone call. Trudel called a female patient of her husband, who didn't have children and adored the boy. The woman quickly collected the child. Trudel gave her some clothes and a note with the address of her friends in The Hague.

Trudel was taken to the prison in Scheveningen. During the first night in her cell she faintly heard a baby crying, which gave her a terrible fright: 'Have they brought my boy here after all?' When the next morning she was given a mug of coffee, she hissed to the guard who brought the drink: 'What's that baby's name?'[45] He said the name of the baby of Aat and Krijn. Trudel also heard that Krijn had been apprehended.

Trudel was clearly in trouble. She was married to an armed resistance suspect. Moreover, she was Jewish. One day all the cell doors were opened: *Juden 'raus* (Jews step out). Trudel stayed in her cell. A cell mate said: 'C'mon, you have to come out.'[46] But Trudel refused. The prisoners who stepped out were transported to Westerbork, where they were taken directly to the deportation train, registered and sent to an extermination camp. Trudel didn't foresee that,

---

43. Interview T. Kolthoff.
44. Breur, *Een verborgen herinnering;* Breur, 'Krijn Breur'.
45. Interview T. van Reemst-De Vries.
46. Interview T. van Reemst-De Vries.

but she refused on principal to be singled out as a Jew. Her refusal to step in line resulted in a severe beating the next day:

> That was terrible. They hit me with sticks. I had been questioned earlier. I'm unsure how long I had been in prison before that questioning. It was at night. They took me to a house. The interrogation was awful. In my presence they tortured an old man. They told me that I'd be tortured too if I didn't tell them what they wanted to hear. One SD man said something I've always remembered: '*Du Sara*' – they called all Jewish females Sara – '*du kommst nach Lublin. Dan fährst du durch den Schornstein*' (you go to Lublin and then you disappear through the chimney).[47]

Trudel thought the German was calling her a witch, who flew on her broomstick through the chimney. She felt rather insulted by what the man had said, but she kept her secrets to herself.

As described, the start of the deportation of Jews from the Netherlands altered the nature of Jewish resistance. Thousands refused to turn up for deportation. Despite enormous problems, one out of every five Jews went into hiding to avoid being taken away. Many of them received help from Jewish individuals and small groups. The Oosteinde group of Ter and Nol turned their political motivated care for refugees and opponents of National Socialism into the rescue of Jews and assistance of those in hiding, an example of defensive Jewish resistance. They used Jewish Council positions and facilities to build shelters and workshops, for instance, to start forging documents. Through their contacts with non-Jews in the police and registry, groups like Oosteinde also obtained personal papers and ration cards and coupons. The discipline and secrecy they were used to was now applied to help greater numbers of people in hiding. Although, as Sera Anstadt experienced, the demanded strictness and obedience were not always beneficial.

People, such as Juud Oostenbroek, often started to help one individual, which was followed by requests for assistance from many others. As these individuals involved family members and friends, small groups came into being. Several Jewish groups and individuals were active in the rescue and care work. Their motives were diverse. The Palestine Pioneers, lead in Loosdrecht by dedicated Zionists such as Joachim Simon, Menachem Pinkhof and Mirjam Waterman, also helped the people escape to neutral or Allied territory. Their work required strong characters and the tenacity personified by Shushu. The individual rescuers and carers mentioned in this chapter included Jacques van de Kar, who had resisted well before the deportation started, and Walter

---

47. Interview T. van Reemst-De Vries.

Süskind, who operated in a deportation collection centre. People were rescued from these centres in many different manners, but not everybody could escape; only limited numbers managed to get away. Knowingly, the rescuers and carers themselves constantly risked betrayal and arrest, but they wanted to help the people who shared their fate.

The deportations eventually also caused Trudel van Reemst-de Vries to be sent to Westerbork, in her case from the prison in Scheveningen and via the offices of the Jewish Council in The Hague. She found it lovely and warm in the Council premises and was given something to eat. Trudel thought about escaping and asked if she could go to the toilet, but a Dutch policeman accompanied her. He posted himself in front of the door. Another officer took her by train to the transit camp. There, Trudel suddenly felt sick. The next day she reported being ill and was taken to the hospital barracks. And then something totally unexpected happened:

> I knew nobody in Westerbork. A man entered the hospital and I saw him asking the nurse a question. She pointed at me. The man came to my bed and said with a German accent: 'Notto sends his regards.' I got such a terrible fright that the blood drained from my face, which began to resemble the bed sheets. The Germans in The Hague had found nothing on me, but had they now discovered my resistance activity?[48]

---

48. Interview T. van Reemst-De Vries.

Chapter 6

ESCAPE FROM WESTERBORK

The man who visited Trudel van Reemst-De Vries in the hospital of Westerbork was Werner Stertzenbach, who – unknown to Trudel – was connected to the group of Ter and Nol in the Oosteinde Home. Werner wanted to save her, prevent Trudel being deported. To understand whether and how this was possible, we take a closer look at this camp.[1]

Westerbork was located on heathland near old peat fields in the eastern province of Drenthe and surrounded with young woods. The soil was soggy, the climate poor. Dutch military police guarded the camp under supervision of the SS. It was a chaotic collection centre for deported Jews. Often thousands were forced to live in an area that was far too small to hold all the inmates, squeezing them into wooden barracks. They were awaiting transport to camps in Eastern Europe. The waiting time could vary, as the transport train couldn't take all the prisoners at once. Some of them tried to prolong their stay, others hoped for cancellation of their transport, most tried and hoped in vain. A nervous tension held the inmates in its grip, especially on the eve of the transport train leaving the camp.

Jewish refugees had been incarcerated in Westerbork before the deportation started in July 1942, several of them for more than three years. Before the war, Westerbork had been a Central Refugee Camp, where some of the Germans Jews who were interned in the Netherlands were taken. After May 1940 they had been joined by dozens of others, who were sent there by the German police. These *alte Lagerinsassen* (veteran camp inmates) had been given specific tasks, for example, in the administration building or maintenance department. During the occupation of the Netherlands the German Jews were often the first targets of National Socialist persecution, but this also resulted in some of them, such as the *alte Lagerinsassen* of Westerbork, gaining positions with seemed to offer some power. It enforced the distrust between Dutch and

---

1. NIOD 249-0250i; Presser, *Ondergang*, vol. II, 287–380. See also Boas, *Boulevard des Misères*.

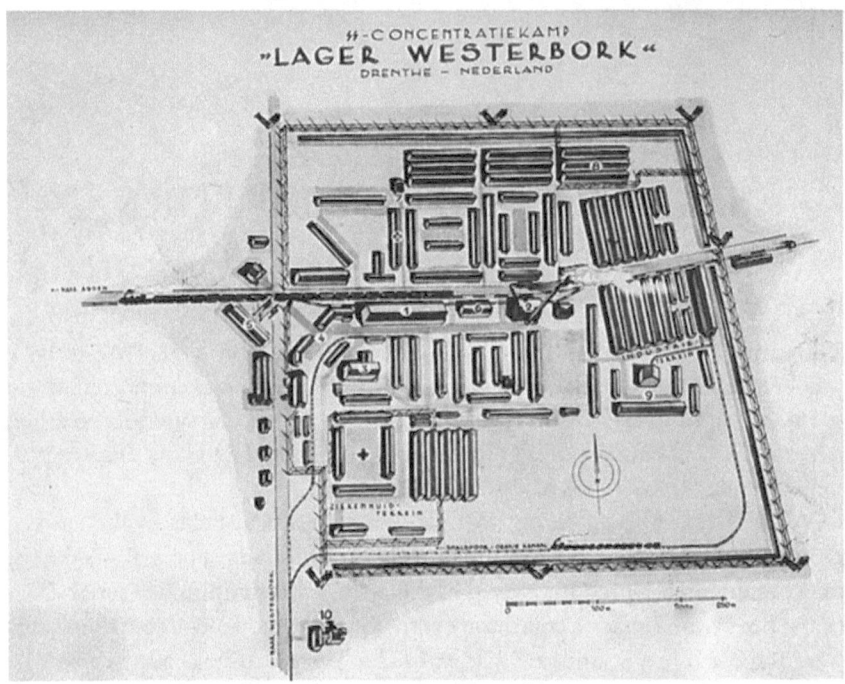

Illustration 6. A map of Westerbork after the railway line had been extended to the camp: 1. kitchen, 2. boiler house, 3. registration, 4. administration, 5. command post, 6. bath house, 7. prison, 8. punishment barracks, 9. workshops and 10. crematorium.

German Jews. However, some German Jews, such as Werner Stertzenbach – the man who visited Trudel in hospital – used their positions to help others.

Life in Westerbork is difficult to understand from a present-day point of view, but you get a glimpse from a series of poems composed by Rosa 'Rosey' Pool,[2] a woman from the Oosteinde group in Amsterdam. She travelled occasionally to the camp for the Jewish Council, possibly to arrange the education of children who stayed there (earlier her poem *The Mark* about the 1942 introduction of Jewish star was quoted). Rosey had been born in 1905 in Amsterdam. She had joined a Social Democratic youth movement, recited her poems in public and studied – German and English, but without graduating. Instead, she had obtained a teaching qualification. In 1927 she had gone to Germany and possibly worked on a dissertation called *Die Dichtung des Nord-Amerikanischen Negers* (The Poetry of North American Negroes). In 1939 she had returned to the Netherlands and got involved with the group in the Oosteinde Home, where

---

2. Geerlings, 'Survivor, Agitator'.

she taught refugees Dutch and English. In 1943 and 1944, Rosey wrote poetry in Dutch and German about what she experienced – *Der Sturm ist Herr geworden* (The Storm Rules). Her poems offer us an impression of Westerbork as the members of the group encountered it.

During the first months of the deportation the camp wasn't yet connected to a railway line. The Jews who had been rounded up in Amsterdam and other places mostly arrived by train at station Hooghalen, from where they had to walk to Westerbork, a journey of several kilometres. During the first months the transports from Westerbork started on foot too, and after reaching Hooghalen the deportees were forced onto a train that took them to the extermination and labour camps in Eastern Europe. Rosey wrote in *The Ride* about an old non-Jewish man with a horse-drawn cart who saw the walking Jews: 'Invisibly a noose hangs around every neck.' The man must have worked for the Germans, because when Rosey rode with him to Westerbork, she guessed his thoughts: 'Your heart knows to pity the "poor Jews"':

> How often seated behind you like that
> I heard the words from your pious mind.
> That's how you soothed your conscience,
> Atoned for the shames of your work.[3]

In *The Last Supper* Rosey described the noisy arrival of deportees in Westerbork:

> Typewriters, a crowd of people;
> Children are squashed and cry;
> Name, place and date of birth
> And the house that you've lost;
> Class, occupation, identity card;
> Baiting, haste, the next one waits;
> Drive, shove and hurry on;
> The machines hammer the lines;
> Passport, barracks number,
> Noise, stink, fear and grief;
> Gloomy hall with typewriters;
> Camp arrival: avalanche of sorrow.

---

3. See also NIOD 246-1024 De rit.

In *Barbed Wire* the subject was the loved ones, family and friends she missed:

> Then comes the hour when the moor could be a sea or a beach;
> The hour that, no matter how much I suffer, still connects you and me.

And that brought some relief:

> Where I stare into the far distance
> Onto you through the dark dawn,
> Where my arms, empty hands
> Believe that I'm with you.
> Then the sorrows vanish with the light;
> I feel your love coming near –
> You know my heart from your heart;
> At night there's no barbed wire.

However, that relief was only temporarily, and during the day she felt lost again:

> The thousands filled with desire,
> They live penned in a small space;
> And millions breathe, eat, read,
> And know not about a barbed fence.

There was the fear about being transported. During the days before a transport the tension soared. Would you have to leave this time? On the eve of the transport the conversation in the barracks halted abruptly when the barracks elder started reading out the names on the transport list:

> The voice sounds from a soulless throat.
> You say with this voice: 'My love'
> And 'You, my child' and a thousand things,
> Which people say when they are people.

It had a devastating effect:

> The voice is just a tool as the many
> Who hear with fear this loud voice.
> The voice knows not of life's goals,
> People know not that the morning glows.
> All the people who lie there have a name
> And have eyes opened wide with fear;

And the voice reads the names, names ... Amen ...
And a thousand know again confusion:
Away from this hell into the new,
Away from this hell, a new goal;
Away from children, away from friends;
The last tie with the loved ones breaks.

Werner Stertzenbach – the man who visited Trudel van Reemst-De Vries in the camp's hospital – was born in 1909, had fled from Germany to the Netherlands in 1933 after being imprisoned for distributing trade union leaflets, but he was extradited to Belgium because of suspected political activity. Werner had returned to the Netherlands illegally and was cared for by the people of the Oosteinde group until he was arrested and interned by the Dutch police in 1936. As an internee, Werner fell into the hands of the German police in May 1940. However, the Gestapo was unable to find proof of his political work, so that he was *abgeschoben* (sent away) to Westerbork in March 1941.[4] As Werner had some experience in bricklaying, he was assigned to the camp's technical services, which built and maintained the sewer system.

Werner's first job was to clear the camp's sewer drains, which were frozen. They had to remove the ice or pour hot water into the pipes. It was a disgusting job: 'We had to pump up all the excrement, so that the sewer could work again.'[5] Later they also found something else in the drains. During the first transports people arriving from Amsterdam were brutally robbed of their valuables. That's why the camp inmates shouted to the newcomers: 'Money *pleite* (Yiddish for broke).'[6] So, many new arrivals flushed their money down the toilets at the first opportunity. It ended up in the lowest point of the sewer, a five-metre-deep sink hole, but still managed to clog up the system. Werner had to unclog the system and suddenly, to his surprise, he found a banknote. More appeared, often ripped in half. Werner fished a lot of them out of the sewer and where needed, glued fragments together and sent repaired and cleaned banknotes to the Oosteinde group in Amsterdam, with whom he had kept in touch: 'They say in Dutch "*geld stinkt niet*" [money doesn't smell, from the Latin *bona pecunia non olet* – good money smells but doesn't stink], but that money stank.'[7]

He was able to send this money with the help of another inmate. In Westerbork Werner had met Jupp Mahler. In March 1940, Jupp and his wife

---

4. HStA RW58: 25501.
5. Interview W. Stertzenbach.
6. Interview W. Stertzenbach.
7. Interview W. Stertzenbach.

Hedwig had been prisoners of the German police in Düsseldorf, but the investigation didn't produce solid evidence. Jupp had maintained he was a Social Democrat and denied all accusations of being a Communist who planned the overthrow of the German government. He had even been able to explain a copy of a letter to Radio Moscow, which the Dutch police had found in his Venlo home and had made its way into his German file: 'I had heard an interesting programme about printing techniques.'[8] He had simply reacted to the broadcast, that was all. Jupp asked his interrogators whether Hedwig and he could emigrate to Bolivia. The German police decided differently and sent the couple to Westerbork.

In the camp Werner and Jupp formed a small group of like-minded prisoners.[9] A Dutch author noted in her diary letters:

Sunday evening 23 November 1942 (Westerbork)

The Mahlers are taking good care of me. It's now half past eight at night and I've returned to their hospitable small space that is an oasis [in the camp]. Stertzenbach's brother is writing letters and will tell us later about his experiences in prison.[10]

They were in contact with the Oosteinde group in Amsterdam and in addition to regular messages, Werner sent the money. In return, the group in Westerbork received falsified documents and other materials. Telephone and mail contact was possible. The camp inmates could receive letters and packages. For example, Werner corresponded extensively with Stella Pach, a Dutch girl who he had met before the war at an Esperanto event and with whom he had fallen in love.[11] However, because of German censors, detection was a constant danger. That was why the Oosteinde group in Amsterdam addressed missives and parcels to a fictitious person in Westerbork: Karel Merksma. Jupp worked in the mailroom and took the post addressed to Merksma out of the mailbags before it went to the censor. Keeping in touch was also possible through representatives and couriers of the Jewish Council, such as Rosey Pool, and other visitors.[12] Furthermore, inmates like Werner and Jupp could on occasion travel between Amsterdam and Westerbork, for example, because the Mahlers were allowed to go to the capital and wrap up their Refaka business affairs.

---

8. HStA RW 58:869.
9. Interviews G. Laske, L. Boll and B. Ast.
10. Hillesum, *Het denkende hart van de barak*, 13, 117f.
11. Pach, 'Estella Pach – Hat verhaal van mijn moeder'.
12. Interview J. Reutlinger.

Werner was warned by the Oosteinde group that Trudel van Reemst-De Vries had been deported to Westerbork. He found her in the camp's hospital. Werner reassured Trudel that they had removed her documents from the camp administration. These papers were marked S, which meant she was a punishment prisoner, who normally received special treatment, was locked up in a separate barrack and put on the first possible transport. Without documents it was relatively safe for Trudel to remain in Westerbork – she was as it were in hiding in the camp.

In Westerbork Trudel gave birth to her second child (her first-born was still with friends). Her brother-in-law, Ger van Reemst, lived in a nearby village. In February 1943 he received a message, saying that Trudel was in Westerbork: 'The second child was born there in May. It only survived for a few days, thanks to the poor hygiene of the camp. My father collected the body. We buried it here.'[13]

Ger van Reemst worked for the National Forest Service. He was acquainted with a Dutch civil servant in Westerbork. Through this man, Ger kept in touch with his sister-in-law. They sent each other brief notes: 'In this way I kept her up to date with the condition of her eldest child. The tragedy was that the child didn't react to sound. It was deaf and dumb. We told her carefully, but it was terrible news for Trudel.'[14]

The forestry work provided Ger with a cover to get close to the camp perimeter. He cycled to a young wood next to Westerbork. There he met Werner, who could get outside the barbed wire fence to repair and maintain the sewer. In this manner Ger became a vital link between the groups in the Oosteinde Home and Westerbork for one aspect of their resistance work, namely helping inmates escape from the camp.

Fleeing Westerbork wasn't easy. It has been estimated that in total just over two hundred prisoners escaped, but this estimate may be too low.[15] In any case, the difficulties were manifold. How did you get beyond the barbed wire? Where could you go once you were outside the fence? How did you get documents, money, transport, food and a hiding place? Could you expect help outside the camp? Was there a lot of betrayal? Who could you trust? In addition, the Germans threatened with severe reprisals. For every detected fugitive, they would put 10 prisoners from the same barrack on a special punishment transport, which offered little or no chance of survival.

---

13. Interview G. van Reemst.
14. Interview G. van Reemst.
15. De Jong, *Het Koninkrijk der Nederlanden in de Tweede Wereldoorlog*, vol. VIII, 738–40; Mulder, Martin, Abuys, *Een gat in het prikkeldraad*; Presser, *Ondergang*, vol. II, 361. A recent overview mentions a figure of 334 escapes (https://meitotmei.nl).

Therefore, Werner and his small group had to arrange a lot and make far-reaching decisions before they helped somebody to escape, which was also complicated by the chaos of camp life and brought risks for themselves in terms of detection and punishment. Werner always asked himself: 'Does it make sense to risk your life?' He had to choose: 'We were anti-National Socialists. For us fighting and assisting people were part of the same struggle.' So Werner asked potential escapees: 'What will you do after your escape? Will you join the resistance?'[16] The candidate for escape also had to be tight-lipped. On one occasion Werner agreed to help somebody, but withdrew his promise after the man told his barrack elder that he was going to escape.

As a rule, Werner could help just one person at a time. He only once made an exception. This concerned a couple. In the dark, Werner took the husband and wife to a sewer outlet. Suddenly he saw an SS officer. They usually didn't come here, because of the nauseating smell. The couple hid quickly, but Werner was unable to avoid the SS man. He showed his pass and told the man he wanted to check one of the pumps. Although the pass was apparently valid only during daylight hours, the officer believed Werner and let him go with the words: '*Ihr Juden sind doch kein richtige Menschen*' (You Jews simply aren't right people).[17] Shaking with dread, Werner found the couple and helped them get away. After that he didn't dare to take the same risk. Individuals didn't require help in such a roundabout way. Werner could take them out during the day, when being outside the fence aroused less suspicion.

Nevertheless, the escape of Bella Przyrowski was far from easy. She had been active in the Oosteinde group and was married to Ernst Levy, one of the group leaders. After her arrest Bella was sent from the prison in Scheveningen to Westerbork. Werner was notified, found her and planned the flight. He made arrangements with Ger. The forester would meet Bella outside the camp and hand her over to a member of the Oosteinde group, who'd come from Amsterdam to collect her.

It almost ended in disaster. Werner and another inmate took Bella, dressed in an overall of the technical service, to a side gate in the fence. Two Jewish camp stewards were posted there. They could be persuaded to turn a blind eye. However, Werner's helper got too nervous: 'The SS in the watchtower has spotted us. They know what we're up to. This isn't working. We have to go back.'[18] Filled with fear, the man was unable to continue. Watched by the guard, the trio went back into the camp. Werner decided to act on his own and smuggle Bella out in a tipping cart, which he normally used for sewer work.

---

16. Interview W. Stertzenbach.
17. Interview W. Stertzenbach.
18. Interview W. Stertzenbach.

Bella disappeared in a sack in the cart. He covered the cart with a slab of stone or concrete, pushed it through the side gate with the Jewish stewards and helped Bella out of the cart once they were well away and hidden from the fence. Werner told her to wait for him here, while he took the cart away. When Werner returned, Bella seemed to have vanished. It took him 10 minutes to find her in the undergrowth. She was almost scared to death. Werner took her to a path, until he could go no further. Fortunately, Bella was expected at the end of the path, where she was met and taken to a hiding place in Amsterdam.

Meanwhile, Bella's husband Ernst was transferred from the prison in Scheveningen to the concentration camp of Vught in the southern province of North Brabant, which occasionally functioned as a transit point for arrested resistance members and Jews. Trudel's husband Theo van Reemst was also imprisoned there, he worked as a doctor in the camp. Via her brother-in-law Ger, Trudel asked Theo to help Ernst. Theo regularly sent body fluid samples taken from prisoners to the National Institute for Bacteriological Research. He had arranged with staff members of the Institute that if he put a dot behind a disease on the form that accompanied the sample, the researchers would give a positive test result for that disease. The Germans were sometimes reluctant to send infected prisoners on a transport to another prison or camp, in fear of spreading disease or causing epidemics. With this arrangement, Theo could occasionally protect prisoners from being deported. He also tried it for Ernst. However, Bella's husband was put on a transport.

Ernst was mentioned one more time in German reports. In 1944 the police in Düsseldorf inquired about him. The German police in The Hague answered that he was deported 'by accident': '*Seine Rückführung wurde in die Wege geleitet*' (His return is set in motion). The Düsseldorf police felt that was unnecessary: 'His further interrogation isn't expected to reveal new clues.'[19] Ernst was probably dead already.

Besides the tipping cart, for some escape attempts Werner used a small lorry, meant to take the bodies of deceased inmates to a crematorium outside the barbed wire fence, for which he was responsible too. He specifically took the lorry if the group had to improvise at the last moment, for example, when they were informed about somebody who had to escape on the eve of a transport. Then they smuggled the person out of the transport just before the train departed: 'That posed fewer risks. The SS in Westerbork had collected the demanded number of deportees, at least that's what they thought, and they didn't count in Auschwitz.'[20]

---

19. HStA RW58: 3931 and 20062.
20. Interview W. Stertzenbach.

Fugitives also got away by other means. Despite her Jewish Council exemption, Rosey Pool, her brother and parents had been captured during a *razzia* and sent to Westerbork. The parents were quickly deported to Sobibor, followed by her brother. Then came Rosey's turn. She panicked and sent a message to Nathan Notowicz: 'Send *Die Eisenbahn*.'[21] The Oosteinde group understood this message. Rosey had often told them about American negro spirituals, songs from the time of slavery, when the underground *Eisenbahn* (railway) was a symbol of the flight to freedom. A group member applied for further exemption for Rosey. That was granted. Later she escaped deportation by disappearing during a permitted trip. A journalist incarcerated in Westerbork noted in his diary:

> Mrs P. on leave to Amsterdam to collect books for penalised Aryans, who will find accommodation in the camp, failed to return last night at the set hour to barrack 83. The lady had been listed for transport 14 days ago, but was removed from the train at the very last moment.[22]

After that Rosey went into hiding and wrote her poems.

Trudel van Reemst-De Vries succeeded in leaving Westerbork in a different manner. She was married to a non-Jew and eventually Jews from mixed marriages were exempted from deportation and allowed to go back home if they were in a transit camp, on the condition that they consented to be sterilised. When the decree was issued, Werner told Trudel she should leave the camp. She left crying, because she felt she was abandoning her comrades.

In Amsterdam Trudel had to report to the *Aussenstelle*. She was ordered there to collect her personal files from Vlaardingen, where she had been arrested. Nathan Notowicz waited for Trudel at the gate of the *Aussenstelle*. She was exhausted and he took her to the Oosteinde Home. A friendly doctor – Ben Polak, a young general practitioner who was connected to various resistance groups – wrote a note, saying she was unable to travel and prescribing three days of rest.[23] After Trudel had rested she travelled to Vlaardingen. There she rung her old doorbell. An unknown man opened and immediately phoned the police: 'To find out whether it was all right that I was free. "Of course," they said at the police station.'[24] To avoid being rearrested, Trudel went into hiding in Amsterdam after returning from Vlaardingen. Her young son was now with her, but after a while the child was sent to her in-laws in Drenthe. Ger collected him.

---

21. Interview A. Stertzenbach-David.
22. Mechanicus, *In Dépot*, 168. See also Geerlings, 'Survivor, Agitator', 89–97.
23. Interview B. Polak.
24. Interview T. van Reemst-De Vries.

The activity of Jupp and Werner's group in Westerbork came to an abrupt end. First, on 19 March 1943, the German police arrested Jupp. He was interrogated in the prison in Scheveningen and after that in Düsseldorf. A new indictment for high treason had been issued against him. This was the result of the arrest of a resistance courier. He had delivered a letter to a woman in Cologne, who told the German police she was an illegitimate child of Hedwig Mahler. She had discovered this before the war, written to her mother and visited Hedwig in Belgium. The courier had asked her for help in clandestine activity in Germany. The woman called Jupp a Communist.

Jupp denied membership of the Communist Party, but this time the situation appeared desperate. Did he realise this? Jupp wrote Hedwig in Westerbork a hopeful and perhaps warning letter:

> I hope that you're well, I'm pretty good, only suffering a lot from my war wound [from the First World War]. I kiss you. Please write back soon, say hello to friends and also give [the woman in Cologne] my address, so she can write me.
>
> Yours sincerely loving Jupp.[25]

The German police read the letter but didn't post it. Instead, a final report conclusion was drafted. The police wanted to eliminate Jupp and recommended: 'Transport to a concentration camp *Stufe III* [Grade III, which denotes camps that were intended to be the toughest for political prisoners].' Berlin agreed on 11 September. It was no longer needed, Jupp had died in prison on 1 September. His death certificate declared 'cardiac arrest'.[26] His wife Hedwig was put on a transport to Eastern Europe.

During that same month Ger van Reemst received an unexpected phone call from Westerbork. It concerned Werner Stertzenbach. At about half past one at night on 21 September 1943, a boy had come to wake him. Could Werner come immediately? That request wasn't unusual, because it was a night before the transport train left Westerbork. Almost at every transport, camp staff like Werner were wakened to try a last attempt to exempt somebody from deportation, deliver food and cigarettes, send a few letters and postcards or collect a last message for family and friends. Werner got up, assuming that he would be asked one of these favours.

However, he was told to light the oven of the camp's crematorium. But why was there such a rush to do that in the middle of the night? In the twilight Werner

---

25. HStA RW58: 3933.
26. HStA RW58: 3933.

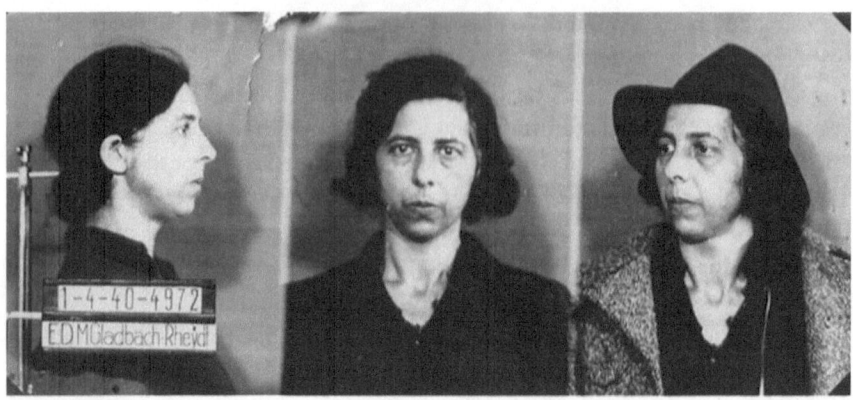

Illustration 7. a, b and c The German police took photos of Hedwig and Jupp Mahler after they had been arrested in 1940. Jupp was photographed again in 1943.

saw a truck parked in front of the crematorium. Inside the building, it became clear that someone had unsuccessfully tried to light the oven. The camp's SS commandant was there too. He said his men would rather have done it alone, but found that they needed Werner's help. The commandant told Werner: 'Before the night is over you must burn the corpses of ten killed criminals, saboteurs and murderers. They've been convicted by a military court and were executed tonight.' He continued: 'You're not allowed to discuss this with anyone. Otherwise …' and he made a telling gesture towards his gun.[27]

The SS had also collected four shaven-headed men from the punishment barrack. They had to drag the corpses from the truck into the crematorium. The vehicle was covered in blood, dripping from the lifeless bodies. The truck also contained stakes, to which the men had been bound for the execution. Werner saw that most of the shot men were young. To judge by their clothing, Werner thought they were peat diggers. Some still had a blindfold over their eyes. The bullets had hit them all over their bodies. One in the forehead, the other in the chest, the next one in the belly. Werner believed he could still read the fear in their eyes.

The SS men, some drunk, didn't leave Werner alone. It became a sinister and strenuous job to cremate the remains of the 10 men, who turned out to have been hostages and members of resistance groups.

On his way back to the camp, Werner saw the transport train being readied: 'The four boys from the punishment barrack, who had done the dirty work, went straight from the crematorium into the train.' Werner realised that he too knew too much: 'After I agreed with the members of my group that they would flee when the camp was about to be abolished, I ran.'[28] Ger helped him to get away.

After being locked up in Westerbork, at the start of the deportation, inmates such as Werner Stertzenbach, Rosey Pool, Jupp and Hedwig Mahler began helping like-minded people who wanted to join their resistance and other inmates to survive and escape from the transit camp. Some like Werner, had started resistance before 1940 for political reasons. Jupp simply wanted to help opponents of National Socialism. Others like Rosey had been connected to the Oosteinde Home and were drawn into the group's camp activities. Werner and his group assisted more than 20 people in escaping from Westerbork and collaborated with almost 20 other successful attempts to flee the camp.[29] In Amsterdam Werner went into hiding above the workshop in the Gallery behind the Oosteinde Home. Nol and Ter were already in the attic.

---

27. Interview W. Stertzenbach; NIOD Arch. 189, inv.nr. 24 ('21 September 1943').
28. Interview W. Stertzenbach.
29. Interviews B. Ast, L. Boll, G. Laske, G. van Reemst, T. van Reemst-De Vries and W. Stertzenbach.

Chapter 7

THE BIRTH OF MARJAN

The second child of Ter and Nol was born on 7 September 1943. They called the girl Marjan. The pregnancy had been unplanned. Means of contraception were difficult to get, but Ter had a diaphragm. However, she found it too complicated to use: 'In these days you didn't discuss these matters with your husband.' A visit to the doctor didn't help. He believed: 'It's all rubbish. You must sacrifice.'[1] Ter contemplated termination of the pregnancy, but she rejected an abortion:

> Actually, I loved having children. I also found it too dangerous for the person who had to abort me under these wartime circumstances. And I probably also believed something like 'damn it, I won't let these Nazis dictate whether or not I could bear a child.'

During the last few weeks of the pregnancy, Nol and Ter had hidden in the attic of the workshop in the Gallery. Their first child, Ruth, was still with friends in Gramsbergen. Nol had stomach trouble. The group cared for him with food, especially milk to ease his stomach pains. It was delivered twice a week. Ter couldn't give birth in that attic. They started looking for a safe place. She heard about a natal clinic in Haarlem, about 30 kilometres west of Amsterdam, where her baby could be delivered. That was impossible in Amsterdam, because she would be recognised and could be betrayed, as many people knew Ter from the time she worked as a nurse.

To erase the trail, Ter first hid at another address. Luckily that was only for a couple of days, because the place was infested with lice and Ter noticed that in the final stages of a pregnancy it's difficult to catch lice between your navel and knees. From that address she travelled to the natal clinic. Marjan was born there in awkward conditions:

---

1. All the quotations in this chapter come from the interview I conducted with Ter Kolthoff. See also the 1980 Dutch television broadcast *Moeder, wat deed jij in de oorlog?* made by Agna Arens, Trix Betlem, Godelieve van de Heyde, Marijke Rawie and Ageeth Scherphuis.

No, that was of course not easy. It went well, objectively speaking, well. But the nurse who was on duty that night, as I found out later, had never been present at a delivery. She was so scared that on the moment I rung to ask the midwife to come, she hid herself. So the baby was born before the midwife arrived and without the nurse being present.

Ter knew she'd have to leave her baby soon:

It was terrible at the time, but it had already been horrible long before that. I remember that when I was breastfeeding Marjan, I said to her or at least spoke to her in my mind: 'Drink well. In a few days you'll get the bottle.' It had to be.

She couldn't stay in the clinic:

On a certain day I had to leave. So I disappeared there with Marjan. The people in the clinic never knew more than 'she must have gone home'. In the railway station I handed Marjan over to her wartime foster mother.

An acquaintance had made the appointment for Ter with an unknown woman, later she was called 'Aunt Paula': 'I didn't know her. But, after all, it was dangerous for Marjan to come with me to Amsterdam.' Nor did Ter know how she and Nol would fare. 'Whether we could go back to resistance work, yes or no. But in any case, it had to be done.' Aunt Paula lived in Haarlem or Heemstede, a wealthy suburb of that town. Ter was confident about the woman, because she had been told that Marjan would get a 'good home'.

Meanwhile, Ruth remained far away with her foster parents in the east of the Netherlands. Ter saw her only once during the war, but that didn't go well. Ter had sent Ruth a picture book about an elephant. The foster mother had explained to Ruth that the book came from 'Aunt Greet' as Greet van der Hoek was the cover name used by Ter in her courier work. Ruth had therefore started to call the elephant 'Auntie Greet'. When her foster mother said that aunt Greet would visit her by train, Ruth expected to see an elephant alighting from the carriage. She had already asked her foster mum whether aunt Greet would actually fit into the train. It was therefore quite a disappointment for Ruth that aunt Greet didn't have a trunk. Ter felt terrible and tried to approach Ruth:

They called her Geesje. We had used to call her Geesje earlier, like a pet name, but I kept making the mistake of calling her Ruth, which the child didn't understand. That was a very nasty experience, although the foster parents did all they could to make us as comfortable as possible.

Ter only saw Marjan just one more time during the war:

> When she was about nine months old. You bond with a child mostly because you're together on a daily basis. And then suddenly, I saw a baby, which I knew was my child, but the bond was missing and I actually felt incredibly guilty.

Ter's recollections illustrate one of the most difficult decisions that Jews who decided to resist had to make. If they were parents, they faced a dilemma, because there were not enough hiding places for entire families: should they go into hiding and hand over their children to unknown helpers; or should they stay together, risk accidental discovery or betrayal and deportation? Ter and Nol solved the problem by separating from their children, so that they could continue their resistance work. However, that eventually resulted in losses they couldn't foresee.

Chapter 8

MURDER IN THE GALLERY

In September 1943 all surviving members of the resistance groups to which Nol and Ter belonged were in hiding. Most of the Jews of Amsterdam had been deported. The Germans regarded the Dutch capital *judenrein* (free of Jews). The transports from Westerbork and other camps continued until in September 1944 just a few hundred Jews were imprisoned in the Netherlands and awaiting deportation.

Thousands of Jews were in hiding in the Netherlands. Increasingly, they were cared for by growing resistance organisations, which had arisen with support from the Dutch population that had become more hostile towards the occupiers as it was ever more affected by German actions and measures, such as executions, rationing, requisition of goods, seizure of means of production (that were then shipped to Germany), forced labour and *razzias* to catch men who tried to avoid the labour draft. The war had also passed a military turning point, marked by German defeats in Stalingrad and El Alamein and the Allied landings in North Africa at the end of 1942. However, for the majority of the Jews in the Netherlands the general resistance groups developed too late, they were already deported and killed in labour and extermination camps or would soon succumb there.

The Oosteinde Home in Amsterdam had ceased to exist as a department of the Jewish Council in July 1943. It was emptied and used as a storage place. Towards the end of the Oosteinde Home, group leader Nathan Notowicz and another member of the group hid important documents, clandestine publications and valuable Jewish artefacts under the floorboards. One of the final days was extremely busy when the paper supply of the Home, an important source for clandestine publications, was secretly handed over to another resistance group. On that day the Jewish Council removed tables and chairs, German agents brought in furniture requisitioned from deported Jews and the other resistance group collected the paper and duplicating machinery.[1]

---

1. Interview A. Stertzenbach-David.

The Oosteinde group now turned the workshop in the Gallery into its headquarters. Nol was still hidden in the attic when Ter returned after giving birth to Marjan: 'That was rather tragicomical. She came from the clinic, her breasts were full, and first she couldn't get through the portal of the hiding place. We couldn't stop laughing. She had to practise to get in.'[2]

It seemed a safe shelter, but this place too had to be abandoned. That was caused by an unexpected event. Further down The Gallery was another workshop, where surrogate sugar was produced. A different resistance group used this workshop for clandestine purposes. That group contained a traitor. After this person was identified – as it turned out later, mistakenly – the group decided to eliminate him.

The liquidation of traitors was a controversial topic in the resistance work that Nol and Ter conducted.[3] One of the groups that had decided at an early stage to kill its opponents was CS-6.[4] The neurologist Gerrit Kastein had joined this group, which was supplied with explosives and different means of sabotage by, among others, the medical practitioner Theo van Reemst. CS-6 was in contact with the Oosteinde group, Jacques van de Kar and others, but it operated independently, just as the organisations of Sally Dormits and Krijn Breur, the already fallen resistance friends of Nol and Ter.

The name CS-6 referred to the address of some of the group's founders, who belonged to the Boissevain family which lived at 6 Corelli Street in Amsterdam. The group also had a clandestine workshop in the basement of the Boissevain home. Initially, CS-6 comprised mostly former classmates from a few schools in the neighbourhood of the Corelli Street and students from elsewhere in Amsterdam, including several Jews such as Hans Katan and Leo Frijda. Hans had been born in 1919 in Hilversum, studied Biology and was an acquaintance of Nathan Notowicz. Hans came from a family that had at least 10 members who were active in resistance work.[5] He was also one of the editors of *The Free Lectern*, a clandestine publication started by students.

Leo was younger.[6] He had been born in Amsterdam in 1923, a son of the economics professor Herman Frijda. Leo was a quiet and somewhat introvert boy, who played piano and wrote essays and poems, some of which appeared in clandestine publications. He had intended to study medicine, but when Jews were barred from universities, he started training as a medical analyst

---

2. Interview A. Bueno de Mesquita.
3. Kooistra, Oostbroek, *Recht op wraak*.
4. NIOD 249-0186a, 249-0170a; De Jong, *Het Koninkrijk der Nederlanden in de Tweede Wereldoorlog*, vol. V, 779, vol. VI, 166-7, 613–4, vol. VII, 730–3, 957–62.
5. Katan, *Geen makke schepen*.
6. Tallentire, *Leo*.

in a Jewish hospital. The Frijda family lived in 3 Corelli Street, but in 1942 Leo moved to the home of a friend and he assumed the identity of her brother (professor Frijda went into hiding, was discovered in 1944 and died in Auschwitz, Leo's mother escaped to Switzerland, his brother and sister also survived the war).

In the hospital Leo met and fell in love with Irma Seelig, a German-Jewish refugee, born in 1916. Irma had two brothers, one of whom had died in 1925, and three sisters. Their parents had a shoe shop in Homberg, but the anti-Jewish boycott and violence had caused her father to fall in a deep depression and he had been admitted to a psychiatric institution. Irma's father was murdered by the National Socialists in 1941 in the Hadamar Euthanasia Centre, her mother in Auschwitz in 1943. Irma's younger sister died in 1944, aged 18. Irma and probably the two other sisters had fled Germany before the outbreak of war. By 1938 Irma was in Amsterdam, where she worked from April 1940 as a domestic help in the Jewish hospital. Irma and Leo slept together, and when Irma became pregnant, she sought an abortion, which was performed by Gerrit Kastein and Ben Polak, the doctor who was connected to the Oosteinde group. Irma convalesced in the home of a mother of a CS-6 member, after which she returned to live with Leo, mostly doing shopping and cooking as well as acting as a courier for CS-6.[7]

In the summer of 1942, Leo abandoned the medical course. He wanted to concentrate on resistance work and clandestine publication. CS-6 was engaged in espionage, sabotage and forging identity and ration cards, for which Leo and Hans stole the stamps required to finish the documents. The group also helped Jews to escape from deportation and go into hiding. But they were anxious to do more and do it quickly. Leo underwent a change of character. According to his housemate, he became 'a caged animal'.[8]

When Gerrit Kastein joined CS-6 in 1942, the main direction of the group's activity altered. Gerrit was most likely attracted to the students' thirst for action. After he had first met Leo and Hans, Gerrit apparently told a friend: 'They're fine. Real baby-faced boys. The kind that always want to prove they're very brave.'[9] They attacked a storage of wireless equipment that had been confiscated from Jews, tried to derail trains summoned to transport Jews from the Netherlands and attempted to firebomb the deportation collection centre in the former Dutch Theatre. With Gerrit in the group, and under his influence[10] – one researcher has stated Gerrit applied emotional and

---

7. Tallentire, *Leo*, 150,159–61.
8. Tallentire, *Leo*, 115.
9. Goudriaan, *Verzetsman Gerrit Kastein 1910–1943*, 145–6.
10. De Jong, *Het Koninkrijk der Nederlanden in de Tweede Wereldoorlog*, vol. VII, 957.

moral pressure[11] – CS-6 combined these attacks with assaults on prominent Dutch National Socialists and traitors.

One of the most remarkable actions of CS-6 took place on 5 February 1943. Leo had just acquired a pistol; the group was constantly short of arms. He and a fellow CS-6 member shot and fatally wounded the Dutch army leader and collaborator Lieutenant General Hendrik Seyffardt, head of the Volunteer Legion of the Netherlands, a unit of the Waffen SS. Four days later Gerrit forced his way into the home of Herman Reydon, a Dutch National Socialist who served as one of the Secretaries General – the heads of the national civil service departments that continued their work after the German invasion in May 1940. Reydon wasn't at home, but his wife was, and she was killed. A National Socialist newspaper wrote:

> [...] the Communist Jew Dr. Kastein, with all the heartlessness of his race against Aryan people, waited by the corpse of Mrs Reydon in the lounge for the homecoming of Mr Reydon [...][12]

Reydon was shot when he arrived and later succumbed to his wounds. Shortly after this action, Gerrit fell into a trap set by the German police. On 19 February, he was arrested in a pub in Delft, a small provincial town between The Hague and Rotterdam. Gerrit was taken for interrogation to the German police headquarters in The Hague, but during the questioning he suddenly jumped up and threw himself out of a second-floor window. He didn't survive the fall.

The remaining group members continued the attacks. Early in April they even started preparations for an assault on the Dutch National Socialist leader, Anton Mussert, but the group was unable to implement the plans. Instead, they shot a representative of Mussert. Leo and Hans also killed a police informant. In 1943 CS-6 conducted no less than 24 liquidations.[13]

This activity was bound to put the police on the trail of CS-6. The competence of the German and Dutch police in rounding up resistance groups had steadily increased. CS-6 and connected organisations were infiltrated by several German agents. In the spring and summer of 1943 most CS-6 members were arrested, including Leo and Hans. During his interrogation and a trial conducted in September in the *Polizeistandgericht* (Police Summary Court) in Amsterdam, Leo accepted responsibility for attacks committed by others who

---

11. Tallentire, *Leo*, 146.
12. *Volk en Vaderland* 28 January 1944. See also *Algemeen Handelsblad* 14 January 1944. According to Ben Polak (interview B. Polak), Kastein was not a Jew.
13. Tallentire, *Leo*, 202.

were still free.[14] The court found that he and Hans were the main culprits. Furthermore, Hans was said to be 'the driving force behind all railway and arson attacks committed by the terror group.'[15]

On 30 September, the German court sentenced Leo, Hans and 17 other CS-6 members to death. The sentence was executed the next day. Three weeks later, eight more group members were condemned to death. Meanwhile, Irma, who had been arrested with Leo, was used as an agent provocateur by Herbert Oelschlägel, a *Kriminalsekretär* (detective) of the SD.[16] Irma had to arrange meetings with a handful of group members still at liberty, who were then arrested by the German police. Oelschlägel was later shot and killed by another resistance group.[17]

Some of the remaining of CS-6 members and their work were absorbed by groups who cared for people in hiding. Relatively many Jews were active in one of these groups, the Identity Card Centre.[18] The Centre was formed by artists and students and connected to Group 2000,[19] which also had a relatively high number of Jewish members and cared for thousands of people in hiding. Among them was Rudolf 'Rudi' Bloemgarten,[20] a gentle giant with blond hair and blue eyes. He had been born in 1920 in Maastricht in the southern province of Limburg and studied medicine in Amsterdam. In 1940 he had been involved in the student protests against the dismissal of Jewish lecturers at the University of Amsterdam. He did some courier work and contributed to the clandestine magazine *Rat Poison*.[21] Rudi was also in contact with the group of Nol and Ter in and around the Oosteinde Home. The student was engaged to Hanny Levy. When the girl was transported to Westerbork, Werner Stertzenbach helped her escape from the camp.[22]

Rudi got involved in the *Rat Poison* group through fellow students and people he had met at the Amsterdam home of his mother, which had been a meeting place for artists, refugees and political activists before the war. At the start of the deportation Rudi went into hiding. *Rat Poison* first appeared in

---

14. De Jong, *Het Koninkrijk der Nederlanden in de Tweede Wereldoorlog*, vol. VII, 959.
15. NIOD 248–17632.
16. Nieuwboer, *Eerzucht*.
17. NIOD KB I 6240; De Jong, *Het Koninkrijk der Nederlanden in de Tweede Wereldoorlog*, vol. VII, 961; Tallentire, *Leo*, 210.
18. De Jong, *Het Koninkrijk der Nederlanden in de Tweede Wereldoorlog*, vol. VII, 716–28.
19. NIOD 249-0295, 249-0295a; Van Tongeren, Admiraal, Veldman, Schwegman, *Jacoba van Tongeren en de onbekende verzetshelden van Groep 2000*.
20. Bloemgarten, Bloemgarten, 'Rudi Bloemgarten – Zorgzaam in de omgang, fel in het verzet'.
21. De Jong, *Het Koninkrijk der Nederlanden in de Tweede Wereldoorlog*, vol. VI, 717.
22. Interview G. van Reemst.

August 1942. In 1943 the *Rat Poison* group embarked on a series of attacks, using weapons and explosives provided by other groups. To avenge the execution of hostages by Germans, Rudi planned the killing of the Dutch National Socialist Jan Feitsma, who had been appointed as procurator in Amsterdam. However, when they rang his bell on 2 February 1943, the door was opened unexpectedly by Feitsma's son, who probably wore the uniform of the *Waffen SS*, and Rudi shot and seriously wounded him.

Another target of the group was the railway line between Haarlem and Amsterdam. Shortly after four o'clock in the early morning of 16 March 1943, Rudi met two other members of the *Rat Poison* group. Armed with explosives and pistols they cycled to the main road to Haarlem, hiding their bikes in nearby bushes. The day before they had selected a spot for the attack. Rudi stayed near the bikes, armed with two guns, to cover their retreat. The other two walked from the road, across the meadows to the railway tracks, jumping over the ditches that cut across the grassland. They let the 4:45 a.m. train pass and fixed explosives to the masts of the overhead wiring. The time mechanism of the bomb was set to 15 minutes. Then they returned to Rudi. Suddenly an unexpected train came by, which caused an explosion. The trio quickly cycled home. According to German reports the damage was limited; the railway line was disrupted for only a short period.[23]

It's unclear whether the attack was aimed at disrupting the deportation of Jews. However, Rudi was also involved in one of the most eye-catching actions of the Identity Card Centre, an assault on the registry office in Amsterdam, which may have been meant to hamper the deportation. The card-index in the registry contained detailed information on Jews in the Dutch capital, including their home addresses, and so the assault could have been intended to sabotage the deportation process. Yet, as the register held information on non-Jews as well, the assault can also be regarded as an act of general resistance. In any case, after two aborted attempts it took place on 27 March 1943. Disguised in police uniforms, which they had received from a contact in the Hollandia-Kattenburg factory, the Centre group members entered the building. They used explosives to blow up the card trays and set fire to the cards. Unfortunately, they were unable to destroy the entire register.[24]

Within two weeks the police arrested eight of the suspected perpetrators and a large number of accomplices. Rudi first managed to escape, killing a Dutch policeman who had come to arrest him, but he was arrested five days later in a struggle during which he punched a German policeman and tried

---

23. NIOD Arch. 077, inv.nr. 11, 249-0097; De Jong, *Het Koninkrijk der Nederlanden in de Tweede Wereldoorlog*, vol. VI, 718–33.
24. NIOD Arch. 077, inv.nr. 11. See also Stuldreher, 'Samen alleen'.

to shoot his way out. At the subsequent trial and in the press Rudi was singled out as a Jew and leader of the group.[25] In total 21 accused stood trial in the *SS- und Polizeigericht* (SS and Police Court) in Amsterdam, of whom more than half were sentenced to death, including Rudi.[26] Awaiting execution in prison, he wrote a farewell note to a friend:

> Today we had to compile our final menu, but my cellmates and I don't wish a deviation from the daily rations. You have no idea how united we are in everything and go to our execution full of confidence. We did what we had to do and are completely reconciled with death. Those who lose their life will receive it back as a sacred possession, only too delicate and too fragile to last long. God is calling – we're waiting impatiently.[27]

After the leader of the Identity Card Centre, Gerrit van der Veen, was arrested and executed, his leadership roles were divided over four men. One of them was Gerhard Badrian,[28] a German-Jewish refugee. Gerhard had been born in 1905 in Beuthen (Silesia). He worked as a photographer. Before the war Gerhard had responded to the persecution in Germany with resistance before he fled to the Netherlands. From the summer of 1942 he was involved in forging identity documents and armed resistance. It's possible that members of the Centre knew people in the Oosteinde group. For example, because Gerhard was familiar with political refugees and their helpers, who before May 1940 had run organisations such as the Wuppertal Committee, chaired by Selma Meyer, the director of the Holland Typing Office. The world of the German political exile in Amsterdam was small; for a while Badrian lived across the road of Selma's mother. It's also likely that the Centre, Oosteinde group and Palestine Pioneers used the same contacts in the Amsterdam registry, municipal authorities and police to obtain personal documents.[29] Many refugees knew each other and asked their acquaintances for help and were thus directed to these useful contacts. In June 1944, the German police tried to arrest Gerhard in Amsterdam. He

---

25. *Haagsche Courant* 1 July 1943.
26. NIOD 249-0097, Arch. 077, inv.nr. 11; De Jong, *Het Koninkrijk der Nederlanden in de Tweede Wereldoorlog*, vol. VI, 728–33.
27. De Jong, *Het Koninkrijk der Nederlanden in de Tweede Wereldoorlog*, vol. VI, 733.
28. Gardner, *The Unsung Family Hero*. See also https://www.gerhardbadrian.nl. This website is maintained by Frieda Voorhorst. I'm grateful for the information she has given me.
29. Blessing, Deen, Prins, *Reisgids voor de Tweede Wereldoorlog*, 162-8.

managed to shoot down one policeman but was hit by a rain of bullets and died.[30]

The transformation of Jewish activity towards more violent armed resistance had in fact started earlier – in the summer of 1942, for example, with the attacks carried out by Sally Dormits. This change can be construed as a response to the deportation of Jews from the Netherlands that began in July 1942. Nevertheless, it was contentious. Some of the most remarkable acts committed by the armed groups mentioned above concerned the liquidation of opponents. Although it mostly involved despised traitors, collaborators and Dutch National Socialists, the attacks were controversial, also because they resulted in further German reprisals, such as the execution of hostages and prisoners. Some resistance groups such as the TD group, in which An de Lange – the girlfriend of Oosteinde group leader Nathan Notowicz – was active, opposed violence, disapproved of the assaults and questioned, for example, whether the shooting of the wife of Secretary General Reydon had been necessary and wise.

The elimination of enemies also caused conscience conundrums among the Jewish members of the armed resistance groups. Cor Verbiest,[31] a Dutch policeman who was involved in resistance work with Gerhard Badrian, has recounted how one day Gerhard had collected him. It was exactly one year after Gerhard's family had been deported from The Hague. He wanted to kill a traitor in that city, apparently as revenge for the deportation of his family. Cor was a bit disappointed in Gerhard. He had known the German Jew as a kind man, who opposed violence. Nevertheless: 'We went there. We had to wait a long time. The man came home. When he was inside, Gerhard rang the bell. The door opened. It would have been easy, but he couldn't fire a shot. So, we just went for a drink.' But even Dutch courage didn't work. They returned to the traitor's street, but Gerhard couldn't ring the bell again.[32]

Many factors determined the decision to liquidate a person.[33] In the attitude of the resistance people involved in the attacks a sense of bitterness can be detected, which was fed by the German terror. In this, the Jewish origin of some of the resisters was important. Because, after two years of occupation, their disappointment about the course of the war and the persecution of their people overshadowed any optimism about Allied successes. And despite their help with escaping, fleeing, hiding and caring as well as their attacks on

---

30. *Mededelingen van de Vereniging van Duitse en statenloze anti-fascisten in Nederland* 30 December 1946; Kwiet, Eschwege, *Selbstbehauptung and Widerstand*, 188,190–1.
31. *Vrij Nederland* 16 October 2010.
32. De Jong, *Het Koninkrijk der Nederlanden in de Tweede Wereldoorlog*, vol. VII, 1009.
33. Kooistra, Oostboek, *Recht op wraak*.

transport centres and trains, they were unable to prevent the deportation. It seemed simply impossible.

The despair caused by this impotence was voiced by, for example, Oosteinde group member Werner Stertzenbach, who wrote in June 1942 from the Westerbork transit camp to his fiancé Stella Pach: 'If you review the situation and possible outcomes, you may well come to the conclusion that we haven't yet reached the nadir of our suffering.' A few days later he added:

> [...] I'm very downbeat [...] I received a message from my parents, informing me that [...] they have left on a transport to Poland. They write that what they've long feared is now happening [...] It's a tragic fate that we all face [...] Yes, we must all realise that our life hasn't yet reached its lowest point.[34]

In his November 1942 letter to a friend, in which the Palestine Pioneer Joachim Simon mentioned the fight 'against fate – even if we'll lose', he also wrote:

> There is so much to do. I do my uttermost to succeed, but who knows, maybe it's too late and then I cannot do what's necessary. Everything is so depressing, sometimes I don't see an opportunity to persist. But you shouldn't think too much. Even if everything seems almost hopeless, we may achieve something.[35]

Such feelings also affected the Jewish members of CS-6. In the poem *What Remains*, published in January 1943 in the clandestine collection *A Fight to the Death*, Leo Frijda wrote:

> [...]
> The small cortege went on ahead,
> And from where a heavy coping stone
> Juts out above the sea, one of them plunged to the ground...
> I have cut short this verse,
> ... but with him the world came down.[36]

Elsewhere he noted: '[...] A pile of bodies barricade the door [...]'[37] And under the heading *Death's Solace*:

---

34. AHKW: 521.
35. NIOD 249-1283.
36. Tallentire, *Leo*, 161.
37. Tallentire, *Leo*, 185.

He has finally bowed down to his fate
And understood that he has lost,
once time had extinguished all his fire,
And on his lips place death's kiss,
And he doesn't learn the reason for his birth.[38]

The despair among Jewish resistance people was sometimes expressed in the extremely violent manner in which they fought against the German National Socialists and their Dutch helpers.

In addition, resistance groups sometimes saw no other option than liquidation, as happened with the other group in The Gallery, which decided at the end of 1943 to kill the alleged traitor. The police found the body in the shopping passage and started a search in the other premises of The Gallery. As it happened, Nathan Notowicz was the only one of the Oosteinde group who was present in their Gallery workshop at that moment. He quickly hid behind a wall panel and heard how the police turned the place upside down and found several hiding places. The search took hours, after which Notto quickly made an escape. However, on his way to a different hiding place he realised that the police had left a lot of material. So, Notto collected another group member and together they returned to The Gallery, where they were able to collect coupons and blank identity cards. At quarter to eight, just before the start of the curfew, the job was done.

However, in their hurry they had left Notto's valuable radio equipment. The Oosteinde group member Iens Oostenbroek returned at night to The Gallery. Her sister Juud heard that: 'Iens – a real daredevil – broke the seal that the police had meanwhile fixed on the door, and saved the radio.'[39] Iens was the last member of the group to visit their Gallery headquarters.

As the resistance in the wider population grew after people were directly affected in their daily life by German actions and the military course of the war reached a turning point, Jewish resistance continued. It had started earlier, as Jews became victims of persecution and deportation. The nature of the defensive work by the Oosteinde group was unchanged, but it expanded. In contrast, the character of offensive resistance altered dramatically. It had started with clandestine publications, forging of documents and sabotage acts, but now incorporated the killing of German officials, Dutch National Socialists and other collaborators. That caused further German reprisals, often the execution of hostages, to which armed resistance groups responded with new assassinations.

---

38. Tallentire, *Leo*, 187.
39. Interview J. Wolf-Oostenbroek.

In CS-6, men like Gerrit Kastein influenced other group members such as Hans Katan and Leo Frijda. These young students – for example, Leo who was regarded as a quiet boy – were keen to act, but now they resorted to murder, which would previously have been unimaginable. Similarly, Rudi Bloemgarten and Gerhard Badrian started to commit spectacular attacks. This transformation was mainly brought about by German terror and the deportation of Jews, which Jewish resistance failed to hamper seriously. However, it should be noted that the anger and despair about the deportations was felt by many, but not all members of Jewish resistance groups responded in a similar manner; people like Joachim Simon, Mirjam Waterman, An de Lange and Werner Stertzenbach didn't reach for the assassin's gun.

Chapter 9

IN HIDING

The German occupation of the Netherlands lasted until well into 1945. Following Allied offensives after D-Day in June 1944, part of the country in the south was liberated by the Allies in the autumn of 1944, followed by the east in 1945, but the provinces of North and South Holland and Utrecht, including main cities such as Amsterdam, remained occupied by the German army until it surrendered on 5 May 1945. The occupied area became an isolated German fortress.

During the final years of the war, the survivors of the groups of Nol and Ter had to remain in hiding. Ter called this 'deep in hiding'.[1] What the group members were thinking and doing during these two years was worded by Rosey Pool in *New Year's Day 1943–1944*:

> There were days, which shed clarity
> On the old year in their own power,
> Which gave it colour and shine despite
> Worry, pain and fear and lethal danger.
> There were days, which like gems
> In dark surroundings and side by side
> Shine like candles on a dark altar;
> Days, which disappeared with you.
> You: who gilded the days,
> Which stand as flowers in the barren year,
> You, who still fills hours with happiness,
> Who courageously, quiet, with a trusted gesture
> Smilingly endured the worst suffering,
> Your departure broke the day's string.

---

1. Interview T. Kolthoff.

There was sadness about loved ones, family members and friends who had been killed, arrested or deported and had already died. In *The Shadow* Rosey wrote about her mother:

> For me you're a never-ending screen,
> Which shows all thought and action,
> Whether I write, or dream, or hurt,
> Or asked for you in fear and despair.

Survival became increasingly difficult. There was a growing food shortage, with biting hunger, and it was deadly during the last winter months. There was bitter coldness, because fuel was no longer available. There was constant dread about detection, betrayal, punishment and transport. There was loneliness. A seemingly never-ending nightmare, wrote Rosey in *Awakening*:

> Another night gone: I'm relieved.
> Gone hurting suspicion, certainty;
> Carts are coming down the street,
> In the dusk a flower hangs as ripe fruit.
> The struggle between wake and sleep is fought,
> I celebrate my relief with a deep sigh,
> Colours arise in the morning sky,
> I always know the sombre reason of my dream.
> The light is odd, I didn't see it like this at home,
> On strange walls I see strange pictures,
> Strange noises announce the day,
> People are coming down the strange streets,
> Which I cannot walk in daylight;
> I'm going to let the sunshine in.

But the liberation from occupation and persecution took long. On New Year's Eve 1944–1945 Rosey wrote *New Year's Triptych*:

> Now New Year approaches through the cold hell.
> His feet trip on every step over the traces, which
> The battle left next to gaping grenade holes.
> And the face of every person it meets
> Shows deprivation and hate and hunger.

If you weren't hiding on your own, you could have fun with others, usually in the form of black humour. Oosteinde group members Uschi Littmann and her husband Max Rubinstein laughed a lot. At night, when they went to bed, she wore an old pair of waiter's trousers and he a ladies' dress with short, coloured sleeves: 'We didn't have any clothes at all.' Or if they were fed up with the surrogate food, the pancakes made of sugar beet flew against the walls. And if they had to go outdoors: 'Max once cleaned the windows with a scarf around his head – like a woman. He was afraid the neighbours would see a man. After all, they had almost all been sent to Germany.'[2]

At this time Uschi only saw her sister Gerda in the evenings, on the darkened streets. Gerda purposefully dressed showy, so that she resembled a prostitute, who wouldn't look out of place at night. On one occasion this caused panic when a German soldier attempted to procure her. She quickly walked away.

Nol was also got caught up in an odd situation. One day he was running through town with a laden pushcart – for him, a sure sign of a person in hiding who was moving from one shelter to another. On a bridge across one of the canals he met his friend Hans Wolf: 'With exactly the same pushcart.'[3] Fortunately, they could laugh about the coincidence and the risk they were taking. However, Nol was unable to get out more often, because he didn't have properly falsified documents. During the final years of the war, Nol mostly worked indoors on new ideas for furniture and interior design.

The Oosteinde group members who were able to go out had possibilities to continue participating in resistance activities. Couriers such as Ter delivered clandestine newspapers and magazines. The women also spread news they had heard on the Allied radio. For this purpose, the broadcasts were transcribed and typed out by Gerda Littmann. The duplicated type-sheets, which also contained news and articles produced by groups members, were distributed by the couriers. Eventually, in October 1944 they got involved in publishing the clandestine *Mitteilungsblatt der Interessengemeinschaft antifaschistischer Deutscher* (Information Bulletin of the Community of Anti-Fascist Germans, later *Vereinigung Deutscher und Staatenloser Antifaschisten in de Niederlanden* – Association of German and Stateless Anti-Fascists in the Netherlands). It was one of the clandestine publications produced by groups of German Jews. The Hollandgruppe Freies Deutschland was another such group (illustration 8).

Like Ter, Trudel van Reemst-De Vries operated as a courier from a house in Amsterdam, where other groups members were in hiding too. First, she had slept in different places, but after a while she settled in the Second Jacob van Campen Street, just south of the centre of Amsterdam, where others had gone after they had to leave The Gallery. Trudel was known in the neighbourhood as 'the nurse' because she wore a nurse's uniform, which was part

---

2. Interview M. Rubinstein and U. Rubinstein-Littmann.
3. Interview A. Bueno de Mesquita.

Illustration 8. The Hollandgruppe Freies Deutschland organised puppet shows for people in hiding: *Das gefesselte Theater* (Theatre in Chains). This image was on the front cover of a booklet with a play written by Grete Weil.

of her cover as the fictitious 'Loes van Worcum'. Trudel cycled through the city in her uniform, and was unlikely to be stopped until she was called in by strangers to assist during a delivery: 'The grateful parents called the baby girl after me, little Loes.'[4]

---

4. Interview T. van Reemst-De Vries.

Group leader Nathan Notowicz had another shelter. He was hiding with people who were connected to the clandestine publication *The Free Lectern*. Notto wasn't afraid of going out, taking clandestine materials, even in the dark. On such a night the police stopped him. Notto had a false Honduran passport and managed to talk his way out of being arrested for breaching the curfew. He told the policemen that he was a musician and that the canals at night inspired him. A strange story, but they believed him. And they didn't search Notto. He told his friends: 'These National Socialists are *mesjogge* [crazy].'[5]

Nol and Ter found themselves another shelter, in a street near the Leiden Square in the centre of Amsterdam. There they were informed about the others who had gone into hiding. Occasionally, the group's courier Juud Oostenbroek could tell Nol and Ter how their daughters Ruth and Marjan were doing, after she had visited the children.

In August 1944, the police raided the house where Ter and Nol were hiding. They were looking for print equipment, which had been installed by another group in the flat below the floor on which Nol and Ter lived. Juud had just come to bring them their ration coupons. At the first sound of the raid, Nol went into his hiding place. Ter and Juud didn't have to hide, because they had 'real' or properly falsified personal documents. However, the police searched Juud's bag and found coupons – 'far too many for a single woman',[6] and they hadn't even discovered all the coupons hidden in her bag.

Juud was taken to the police station: 'There I quickly ate all the remaining coupons. I told the police I had bought coupons on the black market. They didn't believe me. They asked how much I had paid for them. But I was unaware of the going rate.' She was locked up in a prison in Amsterdam-South, but was released four weeks later when the prison was evacuated. Prisoners suspected of resistance activity and heavy criminals were sent to the concentration camp in Vught, the others were allowed to go home. Perhaps there was another reason for clemency. Juud was pregnant; her first child was born in January 1945. It was delivered in the former Oosteinde Home, which had started operating as a health clinic. After the birth, Juud ceased working as a courier, but people were still hiding in her home. It was a very difficult time, especially because of the now widespread and severe food and fuel shortages – during the winter of 1944–1945 about 22,000 Dutch people succumbed to hunger and cold: 'I had to queue for hours at a soup kitchen. Near us people were dying in the street.'[7]

---

5. Interviews A. Bueno de Mesquita and T. Kolthoff.
6. Interview J. Wolf-Oostenbroek.
7. Interview J. Wolf-Oostenbroek.

Following the raid, Nol and Ter had to find another shelter. For that reason they split up. Nol also had stomach trouble again. They took him to associates of another resistance group, possible *The Free Lectern*. In their home he slept on the sofa:

> Suddenly a young woman entered the lounge. She left a little while later. When she was at the door of the room, I suddenly said, without knowing why: 'If I ever remarry, it will be with you.' I don't know why I said that. After all, I was happily married.[8]

The woman was Hansje van Wijk. Nol's prediction would become reality later.

Before that happened Nol and Ter got together again in a house on a canal near the old Jewish neighbourhood in Amsterdam. Nol's mother was already hiding there. They got company from Nol's sister Mathilde, Max Rubinstein, Uschi and Gerda Littmann. Eventually, Floor Przyrowski came there too. The girl had serious problems. They had started when Floor had to leave her hiding place in Amsterdam-West. She was too nervous. The group took her to a Protestant minister in Friesland, a northern province. His wife quickly found that Floor was 'more than a handful'.[9] She had to go. The next shelter was provided by a schoolteacher in the middle of the country. She couldn't stay there long either – back to Amsterdam, Friesland again and Amsterdam once more.

One of Floor's problems was that in hiding she missed contact with her peers. She was young and constantly in the company of much older people. With whom could the girl discuss her predicament? Her mum and dad were deported. Her sister was in hiding, Floor didn't know where. She was scared to speak to strangers, couldn't open up about what went on in her head. Finally, Ter solved the problem by bringing Floor into their hiding place and taking care of her as if she was her own child.

Ter and Nol's care group became part of a wider federation of resistance organisations, the Free Groups Amsterdam. The Free Groups had been established in 1944 to connect rescue and care organisations like the Oosteinde group. They were mostly small units, such as the Rolls Royce group[10] of former CS-6 members and the economics student Henk van Gelderen, who had refused to register as a Jew in 1941. Another example was Porgel and Porulan,[11] an organisation of about 20 persons who had started hiding

---

8. Interview A. Bueno de Mesquita.
9. Interview T. Kolthoff.
10. NIOD Arch. 189.
11. NIOD Arch.189, 248-2062, 249-1315; Gompes, 'Bob van Amerongen en Jan Helmelrijk', 21–8; Gompes, *Fatsoenlijk land*.

politically active family members in 1941 and after July 1942 cared for Jewish family members who wanted to avoid deportation. Their work required false documents, which the group started to produce, while it was also connected to the Identity Card Centre. It appeared later that the Free Groups work was conducted by 344 people in 41 groups; one in five of these illegal workers was Jewish.

The people of the Free Groups refused to join the new *Landelijke Organisatie voor Hulp aan Onderduikers* (National Organisation for Help to People in Hiding, LO), because they felt it was 'too centralistic'; that is to say, in their opinion the LO dealt too light-heartedly with the security of people in hiding and their helpers.[12] Furthermore, the LO was not specialised in hiding Jews. And people such as Ter and Nol had been active in resistance much longer than the national organisers and refused to accept the leadership of the newcomers. The Free Groups encouraged cooperation, exchange of news and information, and trade in falsified documents, which were constantly improved. Moreover, they assisted in the acquisition of food, which had become scarce.

Within the framework of the Free Groups, the Oosteinde group was also known as the 'Group Van Dien', which was able to develop a small-scale offensive. Nol and Ter's German friends produced a pamphlet aimed at German soldiers in the Netherlands, calling them to desert. The group distributed the pamphlet. With the growing number of Allied victories, this publication started to produce results, and in addition to several hundred Jews, the Oosteinde group began caring for a small number of German deserters in hiding.[13]

However, to find sufficient hiding places and more food the group had to ask for help from the LO, which caused problems, for example, when one of the group leaders, Alice Heymann-David who spoke Dutch with a German accent, attempted to contact a national official. She was distrusted. First, Alice was blindfolded and driven around in a car. Only after that detour was she allowed to meet the official. The meeting, however, had a positive outcome when the group received financial support to look after five deserters it kept hidden.

Similar suspicion also caused the group problems elsewhere. They produced false identity cards for persons outside the group, but these people weren't always grateful for receiving the papers. For these documents, fingerprints of the relevant person had to be taken with special ink. On such an occasion a meeting had been arranged with the person in a flat in Amsterdam-South. Alice entered the apartment and spoke to the flat owner. The man who had to give his fingerprints was already waiting in the lounge – the person most in

---

12. Interview A. Stertzenbach-David.
13. *Mededelingen van de Vereniging van Duitse en statenloze anti-fascisten in Nederland* 28 October 1946.

danger always arrived last – but when he heard the German accent, he stormed out, saying: 'I won't accept an identity card from a German.'[14]

This mistrust was also fed by anti-Jewish feelings, which grew again during the war, even among people in general resistance organisations. For example, as early as June 1942 the Dutch Communist leadership warned against anti-Semitism and ideas that circulated in the party about Jews failing to resist the persecution.[15] By 1945, from Communists and Socialists to Catholics and Protestants, there were persons who believed that Jews had themselves caused some of the persecution, because they were capitalists who had exploited the working class or had been the murderers of Christ. These feelings increased the gap between Jewish and non-Jewish resisters and hampered Jewish resistance.

During the final winter of the war it became almost impossible to collect and distribute food for all the people in hiding who were cared for by Nol and Ter's group. So they printed small pamphlets, asking people to: 'Invite the children of parents who have even less to your table.'[16] And they shared the little food they could obtain. Nol felt good about that:

> That's the sole thing of which I'm proud. We shared the food between 60 or 70 persons. We were hungry ourselves, but we didn't eat an extra slice of bread. Nothing at all. Not more than we were entitled to. That was poverty. But we didn't steal, and I'm proud of that.[17]

Nol and Ter remained in their hiding place until the liberation of the entire Netherlands. During the long period between October 1942 and May 1945, the work of their rescue and aid group was influenced not only by the uncertainty about deported family and friends, but also by the continued danger of betrayal and discovery, which demanded a constant search for new hiding places, a problem magnified by the hunger and cold of the last winter resulting from the severe shortage of food and fuel. However, as general resistance grew, some Jewish individuals and groups were connected to larger, not-specifically Jewish care organisations, became part of wider networks and made contact with other groups, for example, in the Free Groups Amsterdam federation. This eased their care work somewhat, so that they could successfully hide more people, including German deserters in the final stage of the war. However, they also encountered problems, such as suspicion and anti-Jewish feeling, which had surfaced in some general resistance groups. And this complicated Jewish resistance.

---

14. Interview A. Stertzenbach-David.
15. Galesloot, Legêne, *Partij in het verzet*, 128–30.
16. Interviews A. Bueno de Mesquita, T. Kolthoff and J. Wolf-Oostenbroek.
17. Interview A. Bueno de Mesquita.

EPILOGUE

On 8 May 1945 Canadian troops rolled into Amsterdam. The city celebrated. Was it also a liberation for Nol and Ter? Was this the start of a new and better era?

Following the end of the occupation Ter and Nol had to deal with revelations about the wartime period. For example, the press, including former clandestine papers that now appeared as dailies, such as *Het Parool* and *De Waarheid*, reported about Leo Frijda's girlfriend Irma Seelig, who was arrested and tried in 1948. She was accused of having been 'induced' by the SD detective Herbert Oelschlägel to lead the German police to the 'most important' people in CS-6. Evidence was heard about five people who were caught after Irma's arrest. Witnesses also spoke about awards Irma had received allegedly for this betrayal, including a 'beautiful flat' and clothes, such as a fur coat and silk underwear. In her defence, Irma said she had been 'forced'. The prosecutor demanded 15 years imprisonment. Irma was convicted to 12 years. According to the newspapers, the sentence overlooked that, according to trial reports in newspapers, Irma was only involved 'indirectly' in the arrest of four CS-6 members; the group had been infiltrated by German agents who were involved in the arrests. Furthermore, the group should have been more alert after the capture of Gerrit Kastein, Leo Frijda and Hans Katan. The court reportedly stated that in its sentencing it had 'considered that the suspect would have been executed [by the SD] and by committing treason had saved her life.' Irma's appeal failed.[1] Her former resistance comrades didn't hear from her again.

For a long time Ter and Nol lived as if the war wasn't over. Shortly after the liberation Nol was hospitalised in the clinic which was housed in the former Oosteinde Home. One morning he awoke in the room where the office of group leader Nathan Notowicz had been. A man was bending over him: 'Nol, Nol wake up.' A pronounced German accent. It was Notto. He had come to visit his old friend: 'It was just as if I was back in the middle of the war – Notto, that room, everything was happening all over again.'[2]

---

1. *De Waarheid* 28 July 1948; *Het Parool* 10 August 1948 and 8 November 1949.
2. Interview A. Bueno de Mesquita.

Nol and Ter had been in hiding for so long that they found it difficult to distance themselves from the clandestine existence and return to normality. For example, after the war Ter saw a political associate across the courtyard of a hospital, but when he shouted a loud greeting, she automatically began looking around her to show bystanders that he wasn't greeting her. Well into her late years, Ter was afraid of being detected and arrested, even in surroundings she trusted. On one occasion, she got a terrible fright when somebody touched her shoulder from behind. Ter was unable to continue work and build a career, requiring mental health treatment and becoming dependant on financial assistance and social benefits.

Although some relationships survived, Ter and Nol lost many friends after May 1945. Everybody went their own way. Notto returned to Germany, where he became a leading official in the new regime of the German Democratic Republic. His Dutch wife, An de Lange, followed him with their child. Werner Stertzenbach and Stella Pach had a daughter, but didn't get married. Instead, Werner and Alice Heymann-David settled together in the Federal Republic of Germany. Stella remained in the Netherlands. Rosey Pool first lived there too, but later she left for London. Max Rubinstein and Uschi Rubinstein-Littmann, Gerda Littmann, Floor and Bella Przyrowski stayed in the Netherlands. Sera Anstadt, Hans Wolf and his wife Judith Wolf-Oostenbroek, and Iens Oostenbroek remained there too. Trudel van Reemst-De Vries was reunited with her son and husband, who returned from Dachau. Aat Breur survived imprisonment in Ravensbrück and saw her children again. However, some of these people didn't keep in touch, often because they didn't want to be reminded of the war.

Broken friendship wasn't the greatest loss Ter and Nol suffered as a result of the war. Ter's mother and Nol's brother were dead. Another fatality was their own little family, which fell apart, with Ruth being hurt unintentionally and their second daughter, Marjan, being lost to them for ever.

While Ter continued working at home as a housewife, Nol returned to furniture and interior design. He published the ideas he had developed in hiding in a report called *The Social Function of Interior Design after the War*. He also became one of the founders of Good Living, a movement aimed to improve the conditions of working- and middle-class families through the modernisation of their homes, a concept which had been developed before 1940 in the Netherlands and won support of politicians, architects and artists. Many regarded the improvement as a task to be undertaken by the national government, but Nol wanted designers, manufacturers and distributors to lead what he regarded as the fight against the lack of style, material scarcity and housing shortage. This should result in more responsible choices of furniture and home interiors – functional, sober and light, preferably with plenty day and sunlight. Later Nol designed new products, furniture pieces and systems as well as interiors for offices, companies, hospitality venues and catering institutions.

As soon as they had found permanent housing accommodation, Nol and Ter tried to unite their family, starting with bringing Marjan home.

Ter thought: 'First Marjan at home, because we still have to start bonding with her.'[3] But that didn't work out:

> With hindsight we realised that Marjan was of an age at which you couldn't transfer her at all. She was only two years old, too young to understand what was happening. You couldn't explain anything to her. We stayed for a while with her wartime foster mother. But at a certain moment that child was taken from her safe nest. Later, scientists found that it was totally wrong to have taken her away, and that there had been many problems with children such as Marjan, but we didn't know that then.[4]

For Ruth the change was also very difficult. For a long time she regarded the couple of Olga and Wim Vasbinder in the east of the Netherlands, where she had been in hiding, as her mum and dad.

Marjan's problems were exposed after Nol and Ter divorced on 13 May 1947. We don't know their reasons for separating – Ter and Nol never spoke about each other in negative terms. Later they both remarried and had children and grandchildren with their new partners. After the divorce and the second marriage Ruth lived with Ter, but she saw Nol almost every week.

Ter noticed that Marjan's problems grew:

> It was difficult, very difficult. At first, we didn't recognise that. We thought we should act normally as soon as possible. Just normal. But with hindsight we know that Marjan wasn't feeling right. We noticed that clearly for the first time when she performed very poorly at school.[5]

Nol and Ter sought medical help:

> They spoke to Marjan. And they spoke to us. To come to the point, the doctors advised us to return Marjan to her wartime foster mother – Marjan was eleven at the time. So, we felt that this would be best for her, and we did it. That was of course terrible.[6]

---

3. Interview T. Kolthoff.
4. Interview T. Kolthoff.
5. Interview T. Kolthoff.
6. Interview T. Kolthoff.

Later, Ter questioned whether they had taken the right decision: 'We tried to keep the door open for Marjan, but obviously we went about that very stupidly.' Actually, for Ter it was impossible to discuss this matter thoroughly. The same inability occurred when it came to her other wartimes experiences. When somebody wanted to talk to her about the war, even if that person was one of the children from her second marriage, she acted awkwardly and preferred to remain silent. For example, a daughter from that second marriage asked 'Are we Jewish?' and Ter replied 'God damn it, what kind of question is that? You're like a new Hitler.'[7]

In 1969 or 1970, Ter received a postcard from Marjan saying: 'She didn't want to have anything to do with us anymore. Not with our family. Not with the new family of her father. And not with her sister, who could hardly be blamed.' After that Ter never heard from Marjan again: 'It's very sad. You know that your child lives somewhere and you don't have a clue about how she lives her life, whether she has found peace.'[8] Ter died on 9 June 1990, Nol almost 12 years later, on 16 March 2002. Ruth told me she visited him until the end of his life. Every visit he asked her: 'Have you heard anything from Marjan?' The answer was always: 'No.'

---

7. Interview T. Kolthoff.
8. Interview T. Kolthoff.

CONCLUSION

This book set out to examine the personal circumstances and characteristics of Jews who fought the German occupation of the Netherlands from 1940 to 1945, opposed the National Socialist persecution of the Jews in this country and formed small Jewish resistance groups. It sought to answer the questions formulated by Tydor Baumel-Schwarz, summarised in the introduction, about specific personalities, shared identity traits and common worldviews. For that purpose, this book reviewed what caused Jews to resist, the moment and manner they chose to act, the results of these choices, what influenced their decisions and subsequent resistance work, and who took initiatives and drew in others.

The answers to these questions in this book are conditional and provisional. After all, it's only a case study, focused on a couple – Ter Kolthoff and Nol Bueno de Mesquita – and some of their friends. It's restricted to a limited number of individuals and groups, and there's much we still don't know or understand; so, more research remains to be conducted.

Nevertheless, in general it can be concluded that the invasion of the Netherlands in May 1940 and early German measures and actions immediately caused some Jews to resist. Their resistance usually grew from their pre-1940 activity and opposition of National Socialism, occasionally after they had fled from Germany to escape political and anti-Jewish persecution but maintained a strong desire to act against the National Socialists. Further German measures, specifically aimed at Jews, and the violent acts of Dutch National Socialists against Jews during the first two years of occupation brought about the incidence of different forms of Jewish resistance. The German segregation decrees of 1941, such as the registration order, also caused first steps towards resistance. After that, German terror and the National Socialist preparation for and the deportation of Jews from the Netherlands increased Jewish resistance.

The way in which Jews acted differed greatly. There was no such thing as 'the Jewish resistance', that is, an ideological movement, membership organisation or common strategy. Sometimes people who happened to be Jews opposed National Socialism, sometimes Jews resisted specific German measures. Often, individuals, small groups and loose networks conducted different forms of resistance at the same time. Widely dissimilar reactions to the persecution of Jews emerged and rose, a rise in which Jewish resistance was shaped by general factors such as group traits and social positions which resulted from the integration of Jews into Dutch society. However, just because individuals were members of a specific social group or population segment doesn't mean they always acted as could be expected of persons of that group or segment. And within the Jewish population, people made different choices and the great diversity among the Jews in the Netherlands moulded different forms of Jewish resistance.

To use categories described in the historiography of Jewish resistance, throughout the Netherlands and across its Jewish population, different forms of Jewish resistance can be detected. It was symbolic, polemic, defensive and offensive in character. It didn't include enchained resistance as there were no ghettos and extermination camps in the Netherlands.

The first organised Jewish resistance activities were usually to make propaganda through clandestine publications and protect propaganda-makers and their comrades, family members, friends and others who produced and distributed these publications. During the first two years of the occupation, Jews also protested publicly against German policies and actions. The National Socialist attacks on Jews in early 1941 were countered by boys and men who fought on the street to defend their neighbourhood. Property owners attempted to protect their premises by erecting defences and setting up fighting groups. Jewish workers also took part in the general protest strike of February 1941 to protest against the persecution. The formation of the Jewish Council in 1941 forced leading figures in the Jewish population to make a choice: pragmatic cooperation or upright opposition, and a number of prominent Jews opted for resistance.

Meanwhile, small initiatives were taken for armed action, including sabotage and assaults. The start of the deportation in 1942 altered the extent and nature of Jewish resistance. Thousands refused to turn up for deportation. One out of every five Jews went into hiding to avoid being taken away. They received help from numerous Jewish individuals and small groups, for example, the Oosteinde group and the Palestine Pioneers or Westerweel group, who also attempted to rescue Jews from deportation centres, trains and camps, care for those in hiding, and help them escape.

Much of this resistance had a typically Dutch character, in the sense that it was based on common ideas or formed part of the activity of general organisations where Jews felt at home. Some Jews appealed to shared principles on human rights and authority. Others took the lead in resistance groups that came forth from pre-war political and artistic movements. They also used contacts they had in pre-war organisations of which they had been members, and they looked for fellow fighters, hiding places, false documents, foodstuffs, weapons and explosives among the non-Jews who they had got to know before 1940 in their daily life, study and work.

Nonetheless, Jewish resistance differed from general resistance. It was resistance by victims. A relatively high number of Jews took part in general clandestine activity, including armed resistance. But sometimes they operated separately, like the Oosteinde group, or were inspired solely by their own religion and culture, like the Palestine Pioneers. Another difference was that Jewish resistance developed early, before July 1942 and therefore well before the start of the deportations and long before the general resistance grew as the Dutch population was increasingly affected by an ever-growing number of actions taken by the German occupiers. Jewish resistance was fully developed before the course of the war took a positive turn for the Allies.

The variety in Jewish resistance in the Netherlands was sometimes caused by conscious and determined decisions. Some Jews chose the armed struggle. Others opposed violence or were unable to find arms. Some took principled action early. Others were prompted by a specific decree. As a result, Jewish resistance was often spontaneous and poorly organised, if orderly at all. Individuals resisted intuitively or their resistance came from a wish of self-preservation or a will to protect their family or friends. Getting involved in clandestine activity could also be a cumulative process of small steps, as was the case with Henk van Gelderen. By themselves, the early steps may not have resulted from a clear choice to resist. Furthermore, not everyone was able to choose or chose resistance if there was a choice. However, this didn't mean that they endured the persecution passively.

Similar to the rest of the Dutch population, the Jews in the Netherlands had to respond to the new situation that arose after the German invasion in May 1940. They had to deal with general actions and measures taken by the Germans and the outcomes of these actions and measures. They could adopt a standoffish or wait-and-see attitude, as many non-Jews did – with an occasional exception, such as the general strike in February 1941, the vast majority of the Dutch population didn't actively resist the German occupation and large resistance organisations didn't develop until the final years of the war.

However, sitting on the fence became impossible for Jews when persecution affected them directly and instantly. At first, during the registration of Jews that started at the end of 1940, most Jews reacted in the same manner as the rest of the population: somewhat cooperatively, trying to make the best of the new situation and attempting to lead a normal daily life. There was hardly any public resistance and the Jewish participation in the registration was encouraged by Dutch civil servants who executed the German decree. Furthermore, the requested information was already available from the Jewish religious congregations and it only became clear later where the registration would lead.

The reaction changed in 1942, with many Jews refusing to obey the deportation orders. Despite all the dangers and problems, thousands of them went into hiding. Many more Jews would have tried to avoid deportation if they had possessed the means for going into hiding or if they had known more non-Jews who could have offered help. Some Jews escaped deportation because of the activity of Jewish individuals or groups that consisted almost entirely of Jews, such as the Oosteinde and Westerweel groups. These individuals and groups used their contacts in the non-Jewish population and the positions they could occupy in the administrative machine of the Jewish Council for their rescue and aid work.

Most of the Jewish rescue and aid groups developed other resistance activities, such as the falsification of personal documents and the production and distribution of clandestine posters, pamphlets, newspapers and magazines. During this development, associations grew with the participation of Jews who happened to be in the same place at the same time or who had the same outlook on life or who shared a religious view, ideology or philosophy. These associations weren't tightly organised, they usually consisted of overlapping networks of individuals.

Some resistance groups were more tightly organised. Political refugees exercised secrecy and internal discipline. Armed resistance demanded secret preparation and planning, such as the formation of assault units, collection of weapons, making of bombs and selection of targets. However, the Jewish members of the armed groups depended on external contacts among non-Jews to conduct their activities, for example to obtain explosives. In fact, almost all the forms of Jewish resistance described in this book depended on non-Jewish help, not only in armed resistance, but also in rescue and aid work, production of falsified documents and distribution of clandestine publications.

Despite the occasional non-Jewish help, the tragedy of the resistance by Jews – and perhaps that's also why Jewish resistance is often forgotten or overlooked – is that it became obvious in 1942 that it was powerless against the deportation and murder of the vast majority of Jews. Jewish individuals and groups could only save a limited number of people, often not even themselves or their families.

This powerlessness was the outcome of the overwhelming military might of the National Socialists, the growing competence of the German police, the common preparedness of the leaders of the Dutch civil service and other national organisations to ignore the persecution or even to support it, and the widespread indifference and more limited collaboration in the Dutch population. Perhaps, if Jews had been further integrated into Dutch society, if the integration process had not been hampered and partly reversed before 1940, Jewish resistance would have been more successful, the National Socialists would have found it more difficult to segregate the Jewish population segment and more Jews would have been saved by going into hiding. For example, because they'd have been better connected and had more contacts in the non-Jewish population that were needed for remaining safe. Furthermore, large resistance groups and national organisations who cared for people in hiding, where Jews could have asked for help, didn't develop until the final two years of the war. When the general resistance grew, the fate of most Jews had already been sealed.

What predominantly influenced individual decisions to act and the subsequent resistance work were deeply-felt political, religious, cultural or humanistic beliefs, such as Communism and Zionism. However, these decisions were also determined by widely differing personal circumstances and characteristics as well as experience in clandestine work. The formation of the Jewish Council, the growth of that organisation and its role in the deportations gave members of Jewish resistance groups chances to make use of employment by the Council to protect themselves and other Jews, similar to what some Jews did after they had been sent to the Westerbork camp and taken up positions there before the start of the deportation.

The German terror and the deportation of Jews instigated a transformation of the offensive form of Jewish resistance. Armed groups took novel aims, killing German officials, Dutch National Socialists and other collaborators. That caused further German reprisals, often the execution of hostages. And these reprisals were avenged by resistance members who killed National Socialists and others who were regarded as traitors. The anger and despair about the deportations and the failure to stop them was felt by many, for some it resulted in a remarkable change of personality or brought out characteristics in their personality that had remained hidden, but not all Jews and Jewish groups took up arms.

As the German police successfully infiltrated and destroyed resistance groups, the uncertainty about deported family and friends and the continued danger of betrayal and discovery also influenced the rescue and aid work, with a constantly growing need for new hiding places, forged documents, fuel and food, which became urgent during the shortages of the last winter of occupation. However, as general resistance grew, some Jewish individuals and groups were connected to larger, not-specifically Jewish care federations, such as the Free Groups Amsterdam, became part of wider networks and established ties with national organisations, such as the LO. This eased their work but also brought new problems because of suspicion and anti-Jewish feeling in the wider resistance.

The results of decisions to take action and engage in resistance were at the time difficult to oversee for the people involved. At the start of the war, they may have anticipated a quick overthrow of the National Socialist regime and an end to hostilities. However, as the occupation of the Netherlands continued, decisions to resist had direct consequences, which quickly became clear. By the spring of 1941 it was obvious that the German occupiers violently suppressed Jewish resistance with arrests and *razzias*. When caught, resisters faced a quick death in front of a firing squad or a slow demise in prison and, after deportation, punishment in concentration, forced labour and extermination camps. Acts of sabotage and assaults immediately led to merciless German reprisals.

The decisions to resist also caused long-term reverberations, which few people could foresee. The years of extreme pressure, personal loss and exposure to risk in clandestine activity affected many surviving resisters and caused mental problems, which also affected their children and grandchildren. Nevertheless, Jewish resistance saved thousands of lives from the Holocaust and thus helped to prevent the National Socialists achieving their aim of destructing Jewry.

Finally, this study reveals what kind of people took resistance initiatives and drew others into the clandestine activity. A relatively high number of Jewish resisters came from middle-class families. They often got involved in resistance activity through the non-Jews they knew personally or socially, for example, in education, politics and the arts. However, reactions against persecution occurred across the entire Jewish population. Businesspeople, educationalists and legal specialists publicly rejected the idea that Jews could be denied their civil rights. Rabbis spoke out. Working-class Jews fought National Socialists on the street. Employees and managers smuggled people out of deportation centres. Social workers and nurses became couriers and carried arms and bombs across the country. Trainees in agriculture built an escape route to neutral territory. Students co-founded groups that attempted to attack collection centres. A photographic artist, Gerhard Badrian, took over one of the leadership roles in a non-Jewish resistance organisation.

The first initiatives for resistance action were usually taken by strong-willed persons, such as Alice Heymann-David, Nathan Notowicz and Ernst Levy in case of the Oosteinde group. They appealed for help to like-minded individuals, family members and friends, many of whom were Jews who were drawn into recurring resistance work and in turn brought in their own acquaintances. In this way, for example, Trudel van Reemst-de Vries, Hans Wolf, Juud and Iens Oostenbroek were enrolled by Nol and Ter after Nol was approached by Nathan Notowicz. That resulted in the Oosteinde Home and elsewhere in the formation of small Jewish resistance groups, ranging in size from a handful to a few dozen persons.

The actual work in these Jewish resistance groups was often conducted by young adults, such as Ushi Littmann and Max Rubinstein in the Oosteinde group. The Westerweel group depended on youthful Zionists, such as Joachim Simon, Menachem Pinkhof and Mirjam Waterman. General armed groups relied on students and other young Jews, such as Hans Katan, Leo Frijda and Rudi Bloemgarten. They were able to change their life completely, adopt new means of survival and fight the National Socialists. The Jewish streetfighters were active boxers and wrestlers, boys experienced in public brawls and young men with strong convictions, such as Lard Zilverberg.

But Jewish resistance also came from older people, sometimes prominent figures in the world of education, business circles and the judiciary, such as Leo Polak, Arnold Kahn and Lodewijk Visser. Religious leaders, such as rabbis Simon de Vries and Philip Frank, spoke out and acted because they were concerned about the spiritual welfare of Jews and sought to reinvigorate Judaism as they saw it.

Some of the initiatives for armed resistance came from people with political motives, many of whom had fought in the Spanish Civil War or were men with military experience, such as Sally Dormits.

Women played a crucial role, often as couriers who distributed arms and explosives or as leading figures who possessed ingenuity, resilience and determination as displayed by Juud Oostenbroek and Alice Heymann-David.

Initiatives for the rescue of Jews after the start of the deportation and the care for those in hiding were taken by a mixture of people. It contained individuals who simply wanted to help other Jews, such as Jacques van de Kar and Walter Süskind, and persons who adhered to ideologies, such as Communism and Zionism. In the armed groups, determined men, such as Krijn Breur and Gerrit Kastein, persuaded others to commit acts that would previously have been unimaginable for them, including bomb assaults and liquidations.

Some of the Jewish resisters were well-integrated into Dutch society and made good use of their social position and the contacts they had made before the war. In stark contrast, others such as German refugees and Palestine Pioneers were outsiders in Dutch society, but what served them well was their ideology, group solidarity and, in the case of political refugees, experience in taking initiatives and protecting themselves in their opposition to National Socialism as well as the positions they were given in the Jewish Council and the Westerbork camp, where Werner Stertzenbach and Jupp Mahler operated.

However, as they all fought against the odds, faced formidable opposition and risked constant betrayal and arrest, resistance leaders and members alike needed a relentless energy and the ability to think quickly and act swiftly.

They also had to be prepared to pay a heavy price – many of them lost their lives. And survivors were confronted with post-war pain, fear and guilt. For example, Ter and Nol lost friends and family. Their friends had pulled them into the resistance work and they themselves had involved others, and many of these people had been killed. They had been able to save some relatives, but not all. They failed to keep their family together and were unable to repair the family ties after the liberation. All of that caused distress that haunted them until the end of their lives. They wanted to save and protect people, but they lost many, couldn't shield all their loved ones and their children suffered mental health problems.

In short, the answer to the questions asked by Tydor Baumel-Schwarz is that Jewish resisters had widely differing personal circumstances and experiences, but displayed some common characteristics, such as obstinacy. They were driven to action by National Socialist decrees and acts, while their anger and despair about the failure to stop the deportation of Jews from the Netherlands resulted for some in personality changes. They often shared political, cultural, religious and humanistic beliefs, such as Communism and Zionism, but they frequently were individuals who simply wanted to help other people.

There is another aspect of Jewish resistance that shouldn't be overlooked. The tale of a young Jewish couple and their friends and the history of Jewish resistance in the Netherlands told here offer insights into what determines human life and changes the dynamics and course of history.

History is like a dense forest – a mesmerising, living and growing organism. There's light, which reveals paths, but a path you enter rarely discloses the entire wood. The study of that forest isn't an exact science; it looks for patterns and exceptions but doesn't ignore actions taken by individuals, outstanding persons as well as ordinary people, who all give shape to history. Some of these actions appear irrational. The way people decide and behave isn't always simple. It involves interaction between rational and intuitive thoughts, leading to unstructured mental processes. They're often influenced by unsuspected bias, seemingly irrelevant issues and utterly random events that, detectable or not, interfere with the signals the mind receives.

So, individual actions cannot be fully understood without viewing people in their historical environment, but they'll never be comprehended without examining personal circumstances and characteristics – nobody acts independently from the situation in which they live and everybody operates within their own mental framework. When reacting to a specific event or development, people also respond to other events and developments. They use their knowledge and instinct. As a result, they don't act consistently and rationally in their best interest; on the same day individuals can make different choices in a variety of situations from which they not always profit. To adapt a well-known phrase, while history forms people, people also make their own history, but the outcome isn't preordained.

This case study shows that, in the process of history-making, human life is complex and imperfect, not always clear or clean. Often what are regarded as little things or small details make a difference, even when people endure extreme suffering, as happened in the Holocaust. And what determines individual human behaviour more often than not – and changes the dynamics and course of history – is coincidence. It produces deviations from patterns or creates new patterns.

Exceptions to historical patterns appear in the lives of Ter and Nol. Most Dutch people sought to pursue their normal daily life after the Germans armies invaded and occupied their country – the pattern. However, Nol and Ter made decisions that rendered this pursuit impossible – the exception. Coincidence took them to these decisions. For example, if Nol hadn't liked dancing, enjoyed cabaret and fallen in love with a cabaret artist, he wouldn't have made a friend who asked him for help, space in his new home and to 'do something' against the National Socialists. Without this sequence of personal preferences, peculiar situations and individual conditions, Nol and Ter might never have set a foot in the Oosteinde Home and cared for Jews in hiding. Similarly, in another chain of causes that produced unexpected effects, Ter befriended a fellow-nurse, who went to Spain and married a man who was brought by chance to her hospital after being wounded fighting on the Republican side in the Civil War. If that man hadn't been connected to armed resistance groups, it's less likely that Ter and Nol would have carried weapons, ferried explosive materials and made bombs.

The story of Nol and Ter and their friends lays bare the fragility of human life, but it also emphasises life's tenacity. Nol's eyes lit up mischievously as he told me who became his second wife: 'the girl who walked into the lounge where I lay in hiding on the sofa'. Humans wander along paths in the forest of history, they easily get lost but despite their losses, when they find love, people stubbornly cling to life.

SOURCES AND BIBLIOGRAPHY

Interviews with author

B. Ast, 7 July 1985
B. Bluhm, 3 February 1984
B. Bril, 18 March 1986
L. Boll, 12 April 1983
F. Brandon-Przyrowski, 24 April 1985
A. Bueno de Mesquita, 22 May 1985
K. Döring, 12 June 1984
M. Grünberg and M. Grünberg, 13 January 1987
A. Herzberg, 10 August 1983
T. Kolthoff, 25 June 1985
G. Laske, 4 April 1983
H. Meyer Ricard and O.V. Meyer Ricard-Haymann, 29 October 1984
H. Natkiel, 29 January 1987 and 4 February 1987
A. Notowicz-De Lange, 3 July 1985
B. Polak, 27 January 1987
G. van Reemst, 4 April 1984
T. van Reemst-De Vries, 9 January 1985
J. Reutlinger, 9 February 1983 and 12 December 1983
M. Rubinstein and U. Rubinstein-Littmann, 10 April 1985
L. Sanders, 19 March 1986
W. Stertzenbach, 13 August 1984 and 14 August 1984
A. Stertzenbach-David, 12 April 1983, 13 August 1984 and 15 August 1984
L. van Weezel, 30 June 1985 and 30 April 1987
L. Weil, 18 November 1986
J. Wolf-Oostenbroek, 3 July 1985

Archives

Algemeen Rijksarchief: Bureau Opsporing Oorlogsmisdadigers en Centraal Archief Bijzondere Rechtspleging (ARA).
Archief Herinneringscentrum Kamp Westerbork (AHKW).
Berlin Document Centre (BDC).
Collectie Verzetsmuseum Amsterdam (CVA).
Hauptstaatarchive Nordrhein-Westphalen (now part of the Landesarchiv Nordrhein-Westfalen): Gestapo-akten (HStA).

Internationaal Instituut voor Sociale Geschiedenis (IISG).
NIOD, Instituut voor Oorlogs-, Holocaust- en Genocidestudies (NIOD).
Wiener Holocaust Library (WL).

Unprinted primary sources in private collections

Pool, R. E., *In Memoriam Matris*.
Pool, R. E., *De Schaduw. Gedichten voor mijn moeder. Kertsmis 1943–Pasen 1944*.
Pool, R. E., *Verzen 1943*. Gedichte 1943.
Rubinstein, M., *De emigratie naar Nederland als gevolg van de nationaal-socialistische omwenteling in Duitsland*, dissertation Nutsseminarium Amsterdam, 1951.

Online resources

Biografisch Woordenboek van Nederland: resources.huygens.knaw.nl/bwn1880–2000.
Biografisch Woordenboek van het Socialisme en de Arbeidersbeweging in Nederland: https://iisg.amsterdam/en.
Digitaal Monument Joodse Gemeenschap in Nederland: www.joodsmonument.nl.
Joods Amsterdam: www.joodsamsterdam.nl.
Joods Biografisch Woordenboek. Joden in Nederland in de twintigste eeuw: www.jodeninnederland.nl.
NIOD Beeldbank: www.beeldbankwo2.
Oorlogsbronnen: www.oorlogsbronnen.nl.

Bibliography

Abrams, L., *Oral History Theory*, 2nd edition (London, 2016).
Alderman, G., *Modern British Jewry*, 2nd edition (Oxford, 1998).
Ankersmit, F. R., *Historical Representation* (Stanford, Cal, 2001).
Anstadt, M., *Kruis of munt. Autobiografie 1920–1945* (Amsterdam, 2000).
Anstadt, S., *Een eigen plek. Verhalen van een opgejaagde jeugd* (The Hague, 1984).
Avni, H., 'Zionist Underground in Holland and France and the Escape to Spain', in *Rescue Attempts during the Holocaust. Proceedings of the Second Yad Vashem International Historical Conference, Jerusalem, April 8–11, 1974*, ed. I. Gutman E. Zuroff (Jerusalem, 1977), 555–90.
Balthasar, H., Manning, A. F., Vries, Joh, de (eds), *Algemene Geschiedenis der Nederlanden, deel 15: Nieuwste Tijd* (Bussum, 1982).
Bar-Efrat, P., *Denunciation and Rescue. Dutch Society and the Holocaust* (Jerusalem, 2017).
Barnouw, N. D. J., *Geschiedenis van Nederland 1940–1945. De Canon van de Duitse bezetting* (Zutphen, 2010), German edition: *Die Niederlande im Zweiten Weltkrieg; eine Einfürung* (Münster, 2010).
Barnouw, D., Brilman, P. M., *Verslag van het Rijksinstituut voor Oorlogsdocumentatie en de Landelijk Officier belast met de opsporing van oorlogsmisdadigers en andere politieke delinkwenten uit de Tweede Wereldoorlog met betrekking tot de activiteiten in Nederland van de SS-Obersturmführer Klaus Barbie* (Amsterdam, 1984).
Barnouw, D., Stroom, G. van der (eds), *De Dagboeken van Anne Frank* (The Hague, 1986).

SOURCES AND BIBLIOGRAPHY

Bauer, Y., *Rethinking the Holocaust* (New Haven/London, 2001).
Bauer, Y., *They Chose Life. Jewish Resistance in the Holocaust* (New York, 1973).
Bauer, Y., *The Jewish Emergence from Powerlessness* (Toronto, 1979).
Beek, Th. van (ed.), *Noord in de oorlog. Herinneringen en belevenissen van mensen uit Amsterdam boven het IJ 1940–1945* (Amsterdam, 1980).
Beek, T. van, Scherphuis, A., 'Het dagelijks leven. De Vrouwen', in *Noord in de oorlog. Herinneringen en belevenissen van mensen uit Amsterdam boven het IJ 1940–1945*, ed. Th. Van Beek (Amsterdam, 1980), 28–9.
Benz, W. (ed.), *Dimension des Völkermords. Die Zahl der jüdischen Opfer des Nationalsozialismus* (Munich, 1991).
Birnbaum, P., Katznelson, I. (eds), *Paths of Emancipation. Jews, States, and Citizenship* (Princeton, 1995).
Blessing, M., Deen, F., Prins, M., *Reisgids voor de Tweede Wereldoorlog* (Amsterdam, 2005).
Bloemgarten, S., Bloemgarten, R., 'Rudi Bloemgarten – Zorgzaam in de omgang, fel in het verzet', in *Gezichten van Joods verzet. Veertig schetsen van Joden in verzet*, ed. J. Sprenger (Amersfoort, 2020), 94–105.
Blom, J. C. H., 'Nederland onder Duitse bezetting 10 mei 1940–5 mei 1945', in *Algemene Geschiedenis der Nederlanden, deel 15: Nieuwste Tijd*, ed. H. Balthasar, A. F. Manning, Joh de Vries (Bussum, 1982), 55–94.
Blom, J. C. H., 'Dutch Jews, Jewish Dutchmen and Jews in the Netherlands', in *Dutch Jewry. Its History and Secular Culture (1500–2000)*, ed. J. Israel, R. Salverda (Leiden, 2002), 215–24.
Blom, J.C.H., 'The Persecution of the Jews in the Netherlands. A Comparative Western European Perspective', *European History Quarterly*, 19 (1989), 333–351.
Blom, J. C. H., Cahen, J. J., 'Jewish Netherlanders, Netherlands Jews, and Jews in the Netherlands, 1870–1940', in *The History of the Jews in the Netherlands*, ed. J. C. H. Blom, R. G. Fuks-Mansfeld, I. Schöffer (Oxford/Portland, 2002), 230–95.
Blom, J. C. H., Fuks-Mansfeld, R. G., Schöffer, I. (eds), *The History of the Jews in the Netherlands* (Oxford/Portland, 2002).
Bloxham, D., Kushner, T. (eds), *The Holocaust. Critical Historical Approaches* (Manchester, 2005).
Boas, J., *Boulevard des Misères. The Story of Transit Camp Westerbork* (Hamden, 1985).
Bolle, K. W. (ed.), *Ben's Story. Holocaust Letters with Selections from the Dutch Underground Press* (Carbondale, Ill., 2001).
Boom, B. van der, '*Wij weten niets van hun lot'. Gewone Nederlanders en de Holocaust* (Amsterdam, 2012).
Boom, B. van der, *De Politiek van het Kleinste Kwaad. Een geschiedenis van de Joodse Raad voor Amsterdam, 1941–1943* (Amsterdam, 2022).
Braber, B., 'Passage naar vrijheid: de groep-Van Dien: Duitse joden in Nederlandse illegaliteit', dissertation (University of Amsterdam, 1985).
Braber, B., *Passage naar vrijheid. Joods verzet in Nederland 1940–1945* (Amsterdam, 1987).
Braber, B., *Zelfs als wij zullen verliezen. Joden in verzet en illegaliteit 1940–1945* (Amsterdam, 1990).
Braber, B., *This Cannot Happen Here: Integration and Jewish Resistance in the Netherlands, 1940–1945* (Amsterdam, 2013).
Braber, B., *Waren mijn ogen een bron van tranen. Een joods echtpaar in het verzet, 1940–1945* (Amsterdam, 2015).
Brasz, I., Daams Czn, J., Ofek, L., Keny, M., Pinkhof, M., *De jeugdalijah van het Paviljoen Loosdrechtsche Rade 1939–1945* (Hilversum, 1987), also M. Pinkhof, I. Brasz, *De jeugdalijah van het Paviljoen Loosdrechtsche Rade: 1939–1945* (Hilversum, 1998).
Bregstein, P., Bloemgarten, S., *Herinnering aan Joods Amsterdam* (Amsterdam, 1978), re-issued as *Remembering Jewish Amsterdam* (New York, 2004).

Breur, A., *Een verborgen herinnering. Tekeningen van Aat Breur uit het vrouwenconcentratiekamp Ravensbrück en de gevangenis in Utrecht 1942–1945* (Amsterdam, 1983).
Breur, D., 'Krijn Breur', in *Noord in de oorlog. Herinneringen en belevenissen van mensen uit Amsterdam boven het IJ 1940–1945*, ed. Th. van Beek (Amsterdam, 1980), 110–12.
Breur, D., *Een gesprek met mijn vader. Een twintigste-eeuws verhaal voor drie stemmen* (Nijmegen, 2000).
Buijs, P. 'The Werkdorp Correspondence', *Studia Rosenthaliana*, 33 (1999), 200–204.
Buys, A. 'Rosey E. Pool (1905–1971), Poet. Compiled Anthologies on African American Poetry, The Netherlands', *BAFA*, 33 (1995), 17–18.
Cohen, A., Cochavi, Y. (eds), *Studies on the Shoah. Zionist Youth Movements during the Shoah* (New York, 1995).
Cohen, D., *Zwervend en dolend. De Joodse vluchtelingen in Nederland in de jaren 1933–1940* (Haarlem, 1955).
Cohen, D., 'De herinneringen van prof. dr. David Cohen, voorzitter van de Joodsche Raad', *Nieuw Israelietisch Weekblad* 1982.
Cohen, R., 'Boekman's Legacy. Historical Demography of the Jews in the Netherlands', in *Dutch Jewish History*, ed. J. Michman, T. Levie (Jerusalem, 1984), 519–40.
Colijn, G., Littell M. (eds), *The Netherlands and Nazi Genocide. Papers of the 21st Annual Scholars Conference* (Lewiston, NY, 1992).
Cort, B. de, *Van vrouwen, vrede en verzet. Selma Meyer (1890–1941) en haar Holland Typing Office* (Amsterdam 2015).
Croes, M., 'The Holocaust in the Netherlands and the Rate of Jewish Survival', *Holocaust and Genocide Studies*, 20 (2006), 474–99.
Croes, M., Tammes, P., *'Gif laten wij niet voortbestaan'. Een onderzoek naar de overlevingskansen van joden in de Nederlandse gemeenten, 1940–1945* (Amsterdam, 2004).
Daalder, H., 'Dutch Jews in a Segmented Society', in *Paths of Emancipation. Jews, States, and Citizenship*, ed. P. Birnbaum, I. Katznelson (eds) (Princeton, 1995), 37–58.
Dawidowicz, L., *The War Against the Jews* (New York, 1975).
Dinur, B.-Z., 'Problems Confronting "Yad Vashem" in Its Work of Research', *Yad Vashem Studies*, 1 (1957), 7–30.
Dittrich, K., Würzner, H. (eds), *Nederland en het Duitse Exil 1933–1940* (Amsterdam, 1982).
Fogteloo, M., Gompes, L., 'Henk van Gelderen. Telkens een nieuw stapje, ik had géén keuze', in *Gezichten van Joods verzet. Veertig schetsen van Joden in verzet*, ed. J. Sprenger (Amersfoort, 2020), 147–55.
Eman, D. (with J. Schaap), *Things We Couldn't Say* (Grand Rapids, Mi, 1994).
Flim, B.-J., *Saving the Children. History of the Organized Effort to Rescue Jewish Children in the Netherlands, 1942–1945* (Bethesda, Md, 2005).
Friedländer, S., *Nazi Germany and the Jews, Volume 1: The Years of Persecution, 1933–1939* (New York, 1997), *Volume 2: The Years of Extermination, 1939–1945* (New York, 2007).
Friedman, Ph., 'Preliminary and Methodological Problems of the Research on the Jewish Catastrophe in the Nazi Period', *Yad Vashem Studies*, 2 (1958), 95–131.
Galesloot, H., Legêne, S., *Partij in het verzet. De CPN in de tweede wereldoorlog* (Amsterdam, 1986).
Galesloot, H., Legêne, S., Morriën, J., *De Waarheid in de oorlog. Een bundeling van illegale nummers uit de jaren '40-'45* (Amsterdam, 1980).
Gans, E., *Gojse nijd & joods narcisme. De verhouding tussen joden en niet-joden in Nederland* (Amsterdam, 1994).
Gans, M. H., *Het Nederlandse Jodendom – de sfeer waarin wij leefden. Karakter, traditie en sociale omstandigheden van het Nederlandse Jodendom vóór de Tweede Wereldoorlog* (Baarn, 1985).
Gans, M. H., *Memorboek. Platenatlas van het leven der joden in Nederland van de middeleeuwen tot 1940* (Baarn, 1971), English edition: *Memorbook. History of Dutch Jewry from the Renaissance to 1940* (Baarn, 1977).

Gardner, P., *The Unsung Family Hero. The Death and Life of an Anti-Nazi Resistance Fighter* (New York, 2020).

Geerlings, L., 'A Visual Analysis of Rosey E. Pool's Correspondence Archives. Biographical Data, Intersectionality, and Social Network Analysis', *Proceedings of the First Conference on Biographical Data in a Digital World 2015* (Amsterdam, 2015), 61–7.

Geerlings, L., 'Survivor, Agitator. Rosey E. Pool and the Transatlantic Century', dissertation (Free University Amsterdam, 2019).

Giebels, L., *De Zionistische Beweging in Nederland 1899–1941* (Assen, 1975).

Glass, J. M., *Jewish Resistance During the Holocaust. Moral Issues of Violence and Will* (Basingstoke, 2004).

Gompes, L., 'Bob van Amerongen en Jan Helmelrijk – Porgel en Porulan in het verzet. Achteraf begrijp ik niet dat we het gekund hebben', in *Gezichten van Joods verzet. Veertig schetsen van Joden in verzet*, ed. J. Sprenger (Amersfoort, 2020), 21–8.

Gompes, L., *Fatsoenlijk land. Porgel en Porulan in het verzet* (Amsterdam, 2013).

Goudriaan, B., *Verzetsman Gerrit Kastein 1910–1943. 'Een communistische intellectueel van een vreeswekkende koelbloedigheid'* (Leiden, 2010).

Graaff, B. de, Marcus, L., *Kinderwagens en Korsetten. Een onderzoek naar de sociale achtergrond en de rol van vrouwen in het verzet 1940–1945* (Amsterdam, 1980).

Gutman, I. (ed.), *Encyclopedia of the Holocaust*, 4 vols (New York/London, 1990).

Gutman, I. (ed.), *Major Changes within the Jewish People in the Wake of the Holocaust. Proceedings of the Ninth Yad Vashem International Historical Conference, June 1993* (Jerusalem, 1996).

Gutman, I., Zuroff, E. (eds), *Rescue Attempts during the Holocaust. Proceedings of the Second Yad Vashem International Historical Conference, Jerusalem, April 8–11, 1974* (Jerusalem, 1977).

Gutterman, B., *Fighting for Her People: Zivia Lubetkin 1914–1978* (Jerusalem, 2014).

Henry, P. (ed.), *Jewish Resistance Against the Nazis* (Washington, DC, 2014).

Henssen, E., 'Het verzet van links', in *Het verzet 1940–1945*, ed. R. Roegholt, J. Zwaan (Weesp, 1985), 74–101.

Herzberg, A. J., *Kroniek der Jodenvervolging, 1940–1945*, 5th edition (Amsterdam, 1985).

Hess, S., 'Disproportionate Destruction. The Annihilation of the Jews in the Netherlands: 1940–1945', in *The Netherlands and Nazi Genocide. Papers of the 21st Annual Scholars Conference*, ed. G. Colijn, M. Littell (Lewiston (NY), 1992), 63–76.

Hillesum, E., *Het denkende hart van de barak. Brieven van Etty Hillesum* (Haarlem, not dated).

Hillesum, E., *Etty. De nagelaten geschriften van Etty Hillesum 1941–1943* (Amsterdam, 1986).

Hirschfeld, G., 'Niederlande', in *Dimension des Völkermords. Die Zahl der jüdischen Opfer des Nationalsozialismus*, ed. W. Benz (Munich, 1991), 137–66.

Houwink ten Cate, J. Th. M., '"Het Jongere Deel". Demografische en sociale kenmerken van het jodendom in Nederland tijdens de vervolging', *Oorlogsdocumentatie '40–'45. Jaarboek van het Rijksinstituut voor Oorlogsdocumentatie*, 1 (1989), 9–66.

Israel, J., Salverda R. (eds), *Dutch Jewry. Its History and Secular Culture (1500–2000)* (Leiden, 2002).

Iperen, R. van, *'t Hooge Nest. Het waargebeurde verhaal van twee joodse zussen in het verzet, een onderduikvilla in 't Gooi en het onvermijdelijke verraad* (Amsterdam, 2018), English edition: *Sisters of Auschwitz. The True Story of Two Jewish Sisters' Resistance in the Heart of Nazi Territory* (London, 2019).

Jakob, V., Voort, A. van der, *Anne Frank war nicht allein. Lebensgeschichten deutscher Juden in den Niederlanden* (Berlin, 1988).

Jong, L. de, *Het Koninkrijk der Nederlanden in de Tweede Wereldoorlog*, 14 vols (The Hague, 1969–1991).

Kaplan, M. A., *Between Dignity and Despair. Jewish Life in Nazi Germany* (Oxford, 1999).

Kaplan, Y, *The Dutch Intersection. The Jews and the Netherlands in Modern History* (Leiden, 2008).

Kar, J. van de, *Joods Verzet. Terugblik op de periode rond de tweede wereldoorlog* (Amsterdam, 1981).

Katan, M., *Geen makke schapen. Een persoonlijke geschiedenis van joods verzet* (Amsterdam 2021).
Keizer, M. de, 'De CPN illegaal', *Tijdschrift voor Geschiedenis*, 100 (1987), 641–2.
Klempner, M., *The Heart Has Reasons. Holocaust Rescuers and Their Stories of Courage* (Cleveland, Oh, 2006).
Klöters, J., 'Dora Gerson en het eerste emigrantencabaret Ping Pong', in *Nederland en het Duitse Exil 1933–1940*, ed. K. Dittrich, H. Würzner (Amsterdam, 1982), 210–25.
Kochba, A., Klinov, R., 'Het verzet van de Nederlandse Chaloetsbeweging en de Westerweel-groep tijdens de Duitse bezetting', manuscript (in NIOD).
Kohn, M., Grubstein, M. (eds), *Jewish Resistance during the Holocaust. Proceedings of the Conference on Manifestations of Jewish Resistance, Jerusalem, April 7–11, 1968* (Jerusalem, 1971).
Kooistra, J., Oostboek, A., *Recht op wraak. Liquidaties in Nederland, 1940–1945* (Leeuwarden, 2009).
Kristel, C., *Geschiedschrijving als opdracht. Abel Herzberg, Jacques Presser en Loe de Jong over de jodenvervolging* (Amsterdam, 1998).
Kruijt, J. P., 'Het Jodendom in de Nederlandse samenleving', in *Anti-Semitisme en Jodendom. Een bundel vraagstukken over een actueel vraagstuk*, ed. H. J. Pos (Arnhem, 1939), 190–231.
Kwiet, K., Eschwege H., *Selbstbehauptung und Widerstand. Deutsche Juden in Kampf um Existenz und Menschenwürde 1933–1945* (Hamburg, 1984).
Land-Weber, E., *To Save a Life. Stories of Holocaust Rescue* (Urbana and Chicago, Ill., 2000).
Lang, W. de, *De razzia's van 22 en 23 februari 1941 in Amsterdam. Het lot van 389 Joodse mannen* (Amsterdam, 2021).
Laqueur, W. (ed.), *The Holocaust Encyclopedia* (New Haven/London, 2001).
Lazare, L., *Rescue as Resistance. How Jewish Organisations Fought the Holocaust in France* (New York, 1996).
Leydesdorff, S., *Wij hebben als mens geleefd. Het Joodse proletariaat van Amsterdam 1900–1940* (Amsterdam, 1987), English edition: *We Lived with Dignity. The Jewish Proletariat of Amsterdam, 1900–1940* (Detroit, Ill., 1994).
Leydesdorff, S., 'The Veil of History. The Integration of Jews Reconsidered', in *Dutch Jewry. Its History and Secular Culture (1500–2000)*. ed. J. Israel, R. Salverda (Leiden, 2002), 225–38.
Linklater, M., Hilton, I., Ascherson, N., *The Fourth Reich. Klaus Barbie and the Neo-Fascist connection* (London, 1984).
Marrus, M. R., 'Jewish Resistance to the Holocaust', *Journal of Contemporary History*, 30 (1995), 83–110, see also M. R. Marrus, *The Nazi Holocaust. Historical Articles on the Destruction of European Jews*, vol. VII, *Jewish Resistance to the Holocaust* (Westport, 1989).
Marrus, M. R., 'Varieties of Jewish Resistance', in *Major Changes within the Jewish People in the Wake of the Holocaust. Proceedings of the Ninth Yad Vashem International Historical Conference, June 1993*, ed. I. Gutman (Jerusalem, 1996), 269–300.
Mechanicus, Ph., *In Dépot. Dagboek uit Westerbork* (Amsterdam, 1978).
Meijer, J., *Hoge hoeden, lage standaarden. De Nederlandse joden tussen 1933 en 1940* (Baarn, 1969).
Melkman, J., 'De briefwisseling tussen Mr. L.E. Visser en Prof. Dr. D. Cohen', *Studia Rosenthaliana*, 8 (1974), 107–30.
Michel, H., 'Jewish Resistance and the European Resistance Movement', *Yad Vashem Studies*, 7 (1968), 7–16.
Michman, D., *Holocaust Historiography. A Jewish Perspective. Conceptualizations, Terminology, Approaches and Fundamental Issues* (London, 2003).
Michman, D. (ed.), *Hiding, Sheltering, and Borrowing Identities. Avenues of rescue during the Holocaust* (Jerusalem, 2017).

Michman, J., 'The Controversial Stand of the Joodse Raad in Holland. Lodewijk E. Visser's Struggle', *Yad Vashem Studies*, 10 (1974), 9–68.

Michman, J., Beem, H., Michman, D., *Pinkas. Geschiedenis van de joodse gemeenschap in Nederland* (Ede/Antwerpen/Amsterdam, 1992).

Michman, J., Levie, T. (eds), *Dutch Jewish History* (Jerusalem, 1984).

Molema, S., *Beroep: gevangene, de lotgevallen van de Duitse Jood en communist Werner Stertzenbach in de jaren 1909 tot 1945* (Arnhem, 2012).

Molema, S., Mulder, D. (eds.), *Werner Stertzenbach. Rood en jood* (Hooghalen, 2005).

Moore, B., *Refugees from Nazi Germany in the Netherlands, 1933–1940* (Dordrecht, 1986).

Moore, B. (ed.), *Resistance in Western Europe* (Oxford, 2000).

Moore, B., *Survivors. Jewish Self-Help and Rescue in Nazi-Occupied Western Europe* (Oxford, 2010).

Moore, B., 'The Rescue of Jews in Nazi-Occupied Belgium, France and the Netherlands', *Australian Journal of Politics and History*, 50 (2004), 385–395.

Moore, B., 'The Rescue of Jews from Nazi Persecution. A Western European Perspective', *Journal of Genocide Research*, 5 (2005), 293–308. Moore, B., *Victims and Survivors. The Nazi Persecution of the Jews in the Netherlands, 1940–1945* (London, 1997).

Mulder, D., Martin, J., Abuys, G. (eds.), *Een gat in het prikkeldraad. Kamp Westerbork, ontsnappingen en verzet* (Hooghalen, 2003).

Nieuwboer, N., *Eerzucht. Herbert Oelschläger, V-Vrouwen, Miep Oranje, diamanten, parels en goud* (Amsterdam, 2020).

O'Keane, V., *The Rag and Bone Shop. How We Make Memories and Memories Make Us* (London, 2021).

Paape, A. H. (ed.), *Bericht van de Tweede Wereldoorlog* (Amsterdam, 1970–1971).

Paauw, J. van der, *Guerrilla in Rotterdam. De paramilitaire verzetsgroepen 1940–1945* (The Hague, 1995).

Pach, M., 'Estella Pach – Het verhaal van mijn moeder', in *Gezichten van Joods verzet. Veertig schetsen van Joden in verzet*, ed. J. Sprenger (Amersfoort, 2020, 259–72).

Paldiel, M., *Saving One's Own, Jewish Rescuers during the Holocaust* (Lincoln, Neb., 2017).

Peekel, H., Groot, B. de, *Louis Davids, de grote kleine man* (Bussum, 1979).

Pelt, W., *Vrede door revolutie. De CPN tijdens het Molotov-Ribbentrop pact (1939–1941)* (The Hague, 1990).

Polak, J. A., *Leven en werken van mr. L. E. Visser* (Amsterdam, 1974).

Pos, H. J. (ed.), *Anti-Semitisme en Jodendom. Een bundel vraagstukken over een actueel vraagstuk* (Arnhem, 1939).

Poznanski, R., 'A Methodological Approach to the Study of Jewish Resistance in France', *Yad Vashem Studies*, 18 (1987), 1–39.

Poznanski, R., 'Anti-Semitism and the Rescue of Jews in France. An Odd Couple?', in *Resisting Genocide. The Multiple Forms of Rescue*, ed. J. Semelin, C. Andrieu, S. Gensburger (New York, 2011), 83–99.

Poznanski, R., *Jews in France during World War II* (Hanover, 2001), French edition: *Les Juifs en France pendant la Seconde Guerre mondiale* (Paris, 1994).

Presser, J., *Schrijfsels en Schriftuppen* (Amsterdam, 1961).

Presser, J., *Ondergang. De vervolging en verdelging van het Nederlandse Jodendom 1940–1945*, 2 vols (The Hague, 1965), abridged English edition: *Ashes in the Wind. The Destruction of Dutch Jewry* (London, 1968).

Rappaport, D., *Beyond Courage. The Untold Story of Jewish Resistance during the Holocaust* (Somerville, Mass, 2012).

Regenhardt, J. W., Groot, C., *Om nooit te vergeten ... Passages uit het verzet van de Palestina-pioniers en hun Nederlandse kameraden* (Spaarndam, 1984), 2nd edition: J. W. Regenhardt,

C. Groot, *Om nooit te vergeten. Passages uit het verzet van Palestina pioniers en hun vrienden* (Spaarndam, 1984).

Rings, W., *Life with the Enemy: Collaboration and Resistance in Hitler's Europe, 1939–1945* (New York, 1982).

Robinson, J., 'Concluding Remarks', *Yad Vashem Studies*, 7 (1968), 197–203.

Roegholt, R., Wiedeman, H., *Walter Suskind and a Theatre in Holland. A Save-the-Children Campaign in the 1940s* (Boston, Mass., 1980).

Roegholt, R., Wiedeman, H., *Walter Süskind en de Hollandse Schouwburg. De geschiedenis van de redding van joodse kinderen 1942–1943* (Amsterdam, 1990).

Roegholt, R., Zwaan, J. (eds), *Het verzet 1940–1945* (Weesp, 1985).

Rohrlich, R., *Resisting the Holocaust* (London, 1998).

Roland, P., *The Jewish Resistance. Uprisings against the Nazis in World War II* (London, 2017).

Romijn, P., 'The Experience of the Jews in the Netherlands during the German Occupation', in *Dutch Jewry. Its History and Secular Culture (1500–2000)*, ed. J. Israel, R. Salverda (Leiden, 2002), 265–71.

Romijn, P., 'The War, 1940–1945', in *The History of the Jews in the Netherlands*, ed. J. C. H. Blom, R. G. Fuks-Mansfeld, I. Schöffer (Oxford/Portland, 2002), 296–335.

Romijn, P., Boom, B. van der, Griffioen, P., Zeller, R., Meeuwenoord, M., Houwink Ten Cate, J. (eds), *The Persecution of the Jews in the Netherlands, 1940–1945. New Perspectives* (Amsterdam, 2012).

Rozett, R., 'Jewish Resistance', in *Encyclopedia of the Holocaust*, ed. I. Gutman, 4 vols (New York/London, 1990), vol. III, 1265.

Rozett, R., 'Jewish Resistance', in *The Historiography of the Holocaust*, ed. D. Stone (Basingstoke, 2004), 341–63.

Sacks, O., *The Man Who Mistook His Wife for a Hat and Other Clinical Tales* (London, 1985).

Sanders, J., *Adje Cohen. Een leven in verzet* (Amsterdam, 2021).

Schellekens, M., 'Op zoek naar Walter Süskind', dissertation (University of Amsterdam, 1992).

Schellekens, M., *Walter Süskind. Hoe een zakenman honderden Joodse kinderen uit handen van de nazi's redde* (Amsterdam, 2011).

Schippers, H., *De Westerweelgroep en de Palestinapioniers. Non-conformistisch verzet in de Tweede Wereldoorlog* (Hilversum, 2015), English edition: *Westerweel Group. Non-Conformist Resistance against Nazi-Germany. A Joint Rescue Effort of Dutch Idealists and Dutch-German Zionists* (Berlin, 2019).

Schippers, H., 'The Palestine Pioneers and the Westerweel Group", in *All Our Brothers and Sisters. Jews Saving Jews during The Holocaust*, ed. J. Tydor Baumel-Schwartz, A., Schneider (Bern, 2021), 119–34.

Schöffer, I., 'Introduction', in *The History of the Jews in the Netherlands. ed.* J. C. H. Blom, R.G. Fuks-Mansfeld, I. Schöffer (eds), (Oxford, 2002), 1–12.

Schöffer, I., 'Nederland en de joden in de jaren dertig in historisch perspectief', in *Nederland en het Duitse Exil 1933–1940*, ed. K. Dittrich, H. Würzner (Amsterdam, 1982), 79–92.

Schöffer, I., 'Een geschiedenis van de vervolging der joden in Nederland 1940–1945', in *Tijdschrift voor Geschiedenis*, 79 (1966), 38–63.

Schouten-Buys, A., *The Marvellous Gift of Friendship* (Apeldoorn, 1986).

Schouten-Buys, A., 'Rosey E. Pool: An Appreciation', *Baha'i World*, 19 (1984), 802–03.

Schrijvers, P., *Rome, Athene, Jeruszalem. Leven en werk van prof. dr. David Cohen* (Groningen, 2000).

Semelin, J., Andrieu, C., Gensburger, S. (eds), *Resisting Genocide. The Multiple Forms of Rescue* (New York, 2011).

Sijes, B. A., *De februari-staking 25–26 februari 1941* (The Hague, 1954).

Sijes, B. A., 'Several Observations Concerning the Position of the Jews in Occupied Holland during World War II', in *Rescue Attempts during the Holocaust. Proceedings of the Second Yad Vashem International Historical Conference, Jerusalem, April 8–11, 1974*, ed. I. Gutman, E. Zuroff (Jerusalem, 1977), 527–53.
Sijes, B. A., *Studies over Jodenvervolging* (Assen, 1974).
Somers, E. (ed.), *Voorzitter van de Joodse Raad. De herinneringen van David Cohen (1941–1943)* (Zutphen, 2010).
Sprenger, J. (ed.), *Gezichten van Joods verzet. Veertig schetsen van Joden in verzet* (Amersfoort, 2020).
Stegeman, H. B. J., Vorsteveld, J. P., *Het joodse werkdorp in de Wieringermeer 1934–1941* (Zutphen, 1983).
Steinberg, L., *La Révolte des justes. les Juifs contre Hitler* (Paris, 1970).
Stone, D., *History, Memory and Mass Atrocity. Essays on the Holocaust and Genocide* (London, 2006).
Stone, D., 'Introduction', in *The Historiography of the Holocaust*, ed. D. Stone (Basingstoke, 2004), 1–8.
Stone, D., *The Historiography of the Holocaust* (Basingstoke, 2004).
Stuldreher, C. J. F., 'Samen alleen. Joods verzet in Nederland', in *Bericht van de Tweede Wereldoorlog*, ed. A. H. Paape (Amsterdam, 1970–1971), 1489–94.
Suhl, Y. (ed.), *They Fought Back* (New York, 1967), reprinted as *They Fought Back. The Story of the Jewish Resistance in Nazi Europe* (New York, 1975).
Tallentire, L., *Leo. A Hero of the Dutch Resistance* (2018).
Tammes, P., Scholten, P., 'Assimilation of Ethnic-Religious Minorities in the Netherlands. A Historical-Sociological Analysis of Pre-World War II Jews and Contemporary Muslims', *Social Science History*, 41 (2017), 477–504.
Tec, N., *Jewish Resistance. Facts, Omissions and Distortions* (Washington, DC, 1997).
Thompson, P., *The Voice of the Past* (Oxford, 1978).
Tongeren, P. van, Admiraal, T., Veldman, R., Schwegman, M., *Jacoba van Tongeren en de onbekende verzetshelden van Groep 2000 (1940–1945)* (Soesterberg, 2016).
Trunk, I., *Jewish Responses to Nazi Persecution. Collective and Individual Behaviour in Extremis* (New York, 1979).
Tydor Baumel-Schwartz, J., Schneider, A. (eds), *All Our Brothers and Sisters. Jews Saving Jews during the Holocaust* (Bern, 2021).
Tydor Baumel-Schwartz, J., 'Introduction', in *All Our Brothers and Sisters. Jews Saving Jews during the Holocaust*, ed. J. Tydor Baumel-Schwartz, A. Schneider (Bern, 2021), 19–24.
Tzur, E., 'Resistance in Western Europe', in *The Holocaust Encyclopedia*, ed. W. Laqueur (New Haven/London, 2001), 550–56.
Vital, D., *A People Apart. The Jews in Europe, 1789–1939* (Oxford, 1999).
Walda, D., *Terug in de tijd. Nederlandse vrouwen in de jaren '40–'45* (Amsterdam, 1974).
Wallet, B. T., *Nieuwe Nederlanders. De integratie van de Joden in Nederland (1814-1851)* (Amsterdam, 2007).
Wasserstein, B., *The Ambiguity of Virtue. Gertrude van Tijn and the Fate of the Dutch Jews* (Cambridge, MA, 2014).
Wielek, H., *De oorlog die Hitler won* (Amsterdam, 1947).
Wolff, S. de, *Geschiedenis der Joden in Nederland. Laatste Bedrijf* (Amsterdam, 1946).
Yahil, L., *The Holocaust. The Fate of European Jewry, 1932–1945* (New York, 1990).

INDEX

Anski 30–31
Anstadt
  Selma 74, 75
  Sera 30–31, 34, 70–71, 74–75, 80, 122
Apeldoorn 13
Arnhem 13
Assen 58

Badrian, Gerhard 107–8, 111, 132
Barbie, Klaus x, 32–33, 45, 46–48, 49
Bilthoven 67–68
Bloemgarten, Rudolf 'Rudi' 105–7, 111, 133
Breur
  Aat 55–56, 79, 122
  Krijn ix, 55–56, 58, 77, 78, 79, 102, 133

Cahn, Ernst 46, 51
Coevorden, Adina van (Simon) 68
Cohen, David 47–48, 49–51
Communism 17, 23–24, 26, 27–28, 29–31, 32–33, 46–47, 54–55, 70, 71–72, 93, 104, 120, 131, 133, 134
Cosman, Joël 40–41
CS-6 (group) 102, 103–5, 109, 111, 118–19, 121

Davids, Louis 16
Delft 104
Dormits, Samuel 'Sally' 56, 58, 76–77, 78, 102, 108, 133
Dutch
  People's Militia 56, 76–77
  Theatre (the) 72–73, 103–4

Feitsma, Jan 105–6
Fokker (factory) 13–14, 46–47

Frank,
  Anne 62
  Philip 37, 51, 133
Free Groups Amsterdam 118–19, 120, 131–32
Free Lectern, The (group) 102, 117, 118
Frijda
  Leo 102–5, 109–10, 111, 121, 133
  Herman 36, 49, 51

Gallery, The 14–15, 65, 78, 95, 97, 102, 110, 115–16
Gelderen, Henk van 38, 51, 118–19, 129
Gerson, Dora 25
Good Living 122–23
Gramsbergen 78–79, 97
Groningen 13, 36, 55
Group 2000 105
Grünberg
  Manfred 65–66
  Marga 65–66

Haarlem 13–14, 37, 97, 98, 106
Hague, The 13, 19–20, 23, 25, 30, 53, 55, 56, 76, 77, 79, 81, 91, 104, 108
Hartog, Annette (Dormits) 56, 77
Heemstede 98
Heymann-David, Alice (Stertzenbach) 32, 34, 49, 70, 119–20, 122, 132–33
Hilversum 37, 102
Hollandgruppe Freies Deutschland (group) 45n28, 115, 116
Hollandia-Kattenburg (factory) 56, 77, 106
Hooghalen 85

Identity Card Centre (group) 105, 106, 107–8, 118–19
IJmuiden 13–14

INDEX

Jewish
　Coordination Committee 50, 51
　Council 46–48, 49–50, 51, 53, 61, 62–63, 64, 65, 69, 72–73, 74, 80, 81, 84–85, 88, 92, 101, 128, 130, 131, 133
　resistance, definitions 1–2, 50
　integration xii, 1, 3, 4–5, 6, 11–14, 15–16, 18, 51, 127–28, 130–31, 133

Kahn, B. Arnold 36, 51, 133
Kar, van de
　Jacques 4, 71–72, 73, 80–81, 102, 133
　Jules 71–72
Kastein, Gerrit 55, 56, 58, 102, 103–4, 111, 121, 133
Katan, Hans 102, 103–5, 111, 121, 133
Kettner, Lilly 66–67
Koco (ice cream parlour) 44, 51
Kolthoff, Mark 23–24, 30
Koot, Hendrik 42–44, 45–46

Lange, An de (Notowicz) 66, 108, 111, 122
Leeuwarden 36
Leiden 55
Levi, Irmgard 'Irmschen' 25–26, 33–34
Levy
　Ernst 31, 32, 34, 70, 72, 75–76, 90, 91, 132–33
　Hanny 105
Littmann
　Gerda 115, 118, 122
　Uschi (Rubinstein) 31, 33, 48, 66, 74, 75, 114–15, 118, 122
Loosdrecht (Loosdrechtsche Rade) 67–68, 80–81

Maastricht 105
Mahler
　Joseph 'Jupp' 26–28, 87–88, 93, 94, 95
　Hedwig (Abraham) 26–28, 87–88, 93, 94, 95
Meyer, Sara Cato 'Selma' 23, 32, 107–8
Mitteilungsblatt der Interessengemeinschaft antifaschistischer Deutscher 115
Mussert, Anton 104

National Organisation for Help to People in Hiding 119, 131–32

Notowicz, Nathan 'Notto' 25–26, 27, 28, 30, 31, 32, 33–34, 66, 70–71, 77–78, 81, 92, 101, 102, 108, 110, 117, 121, 122, 132–33

Oelschlägel, Herbert 105, 121
Olympia (sport school) 40–41
Oosteinde Home 26, 27, 28, 30, 31, 32, 34, 49, 53, 57–58, 64–67, 70, 71, 74, 75, 78, 83, 84–85, 89, 92, 95, 101, 105, 117, 121, 132–33
Oostenbroek
　Iens 30, 33–34, 110, 122, 132–33
　Judith 'Juud' (Wolf) 30–31, 33–34, 56–57, 58, 66, 70, 74, 80–81, 110, 117, 122, 132–33

Pach, Stella 88, 109, 122
Palestine Pioneers (Westerweel group) 18, 31, 65–70, 80–81, 107–8, 110, 128, 129, 133, 135
Parool, Het 50, 121
People, The 27–28
Pinkhof, Menachem 67–68, 69–70, 80–81, 133
Polak
　Ben 92, 103
　Jetteke 36
　Leo 36, 51, 133
Pool, Rosa 'Rosey' 57–58, 84–87, 88, 92, 95, 113, 122
Porgel and Porulan (group) 118–19
Przyrowski
　Bella (Levy) 31, 34, 75–76, 90–91, 122
　Floor 31, 34, 75–76, 118, 122

Rat Poison (group) 105–6
Reemst, van
　Ger 89, 90, 91, 92, 93, 95
　Theo 'Red' 29–30, 54–55, 56, 58, 79, 91, 102
　Trudel (De Vries) 7, 28–30, 33–34, 54–55, 56, 58, 79–80, 81, 83–84, 87, 89, 91, 92, 115–16, 122, 132–33
Reitlinger, Kurt 69–70
Reydon, Herman 104, 108
Ricards, Meyer 45n28
Rolls Royce (group) 38, 118–19

Rotterdam 13–14, 22–23, 29, 30, 56,
    77, 104
Rubinstein, Max 31, 33, 34, 47, 48, 53,
    65–66, 73, 74, 114–15, 118, 122, 133

Scheveningen 25, 76, 79, 81, 90, 93
Seelig, Irma 103, 105, 121
Seyffardt, Hendrik 104
Simon, Joachim 67, 68–70, 80–81,
    109, 111
Socialism 17, 23, 27, 32–33, 55–56,
    67–68, 120
Stertzenbach, Werner 83–84, 87–89,
    90–91, 92, 93–95, 109, 111,
    122, 133
Süskind, Walter 72–73, 80–81, 133

TD (group) 66, 108

Utrecht 13, 113

Vasbinder
    Olga 78–79, 123
    Wim 78–79, 123
Veen, Gerrit van der 107–8
Venlo 27–28, 87–88
Verbiest, Cor 108
Vereinigung Deutscher und Staatenloser
    Antifschisten in de Niederlanden 115

Visser
    Ernst Lodewijk 50
    Lodewijk 4, 49–51, 133
Vlaardingen 30, 54–55, 79, 92
Vries, Simon de 37, 51
Vught 91, 117

Waarheid, De 121
Waterman, Mirjam 67–68, 80–81,
    111, 133
Weil, Grete 45n28, 116
West, Mark van 43n24
Westerbork 58, 61, 69–70, 76, 79–80, 81,
    83, 101, 105, 109, 131, 133
Westerweel, Joop 67–68, 69–70
Westerweel (group, Palestine Pioneers) 68,
    69–70, 128, 130, 133
Wijk, Hansje van 118, 135
Wolf, Hans 30, 33–34, 66, 115,
    122, 132–33
Work Village New Gate (Wieringermeer)
    31, 47–48, 67
Wuppertal Committee 23, 32, 107–8

Zilverberg
    David 'Lard' 41–42, 43–44, 51, 133
    Philip 43n24
Zionism 4, 18, 20–21, 25–26, 29, 36, 50,
    69–70, 80–81, 131, 133, 134

www.ingramcontent.com/pod-product-compliance
Lightning Source LLC
Chambersburg PA
CBHW021144230426

43667CB00005B/250